BILLIONAIRES

OF THE BIBLE

HOW THE FAITHFUL

BECOME **FILTHY RICH**

DR. PETER BONADIE

Copyright © 2025 by Dr. Peter Bonadie
All rights reserved.

No part of this book may be reproduced, stored in a retrieval system, or transmitted in any form or by any means, electronic, mechanical, photocopying, recording, or otherwise, without the prior written permission of the publisher, except for brief quotations used in reviews, articles, or educational materials.

Scripture References:

Scripture quotations are taken from the Holy Bible, New King James Version® (NKJV). © 1982 by Thomas Nelson, Inc. Used by permission. All rights reserved.

ISBN: 979-8-9932128-3-8

Dedication

To every dreamer who knows deep within that poverty is not your portion, to every visionary who refuses to believe that righteousness and wealth are enemies. To every Kingdom builder who longs to fund missions, build schools, feed cities, and leave a legacy of impact, this book is for you.

I dedicate this work to the new breed of spiritual financiers God is raising, men and women who are not chasing money, but answering a higher call to steward wealth for eternal purposes.

May these ancient lessons awaken your modern assignment. *May your hands be blessed, may your heart stay pure, and may your name be counted among those who made heaven visible through their resources on earth.*

Acknowledgments

First and foremost, I thank the God of Abraham, Isaac, and Jacob, the *Author of abundance and the Giver of every good and perfect gift*. Your covenant of increase is the bedrock of this work, and without Your wisdom, these pages would be empty.

To my wife and lifelong partner in purpose, whose unwavering faith and fierce encouragement kept this manuscript moving when deadlines loomed; *thank you for praying, proofreading, and believing in this message of kingdom wealth.*

To my spiritual father and mentor, *Dr. William D. Hinn,* who modeled bold generosity long before I dared to write about it, you demonstrated that prosperity and holiness are not rivals but allies.

Gratitude also to the research team at *Kingdom Life Ministries,* whose late-night fact-checks on ancient currencies helped translate talents of gold into modern-day billions.

To every entrepreneur, pastor, and friend who previewed chapters, sent constructive critiques, or asked, *"How's the book coming?"* your voices echo in these pages.

Finally, to the readers: *may these biblical giants inspire you to steward resources with audacious faith and uncompromising integrity. Your legacy starts now.*

All glory to the *King who owns the cattle on a thousand hills, and shares the profit with His children.*

Foreword

By Dr. Stephen Andrews, Th.D.

When I first heard of *Billionaires of the Bible,* I smiled. For decades, I have watched believers tiptoe around the subject of money, whispering about prosperity while quoting verses on contentment. Yet Scripture never blushed at the sight of silver or gold; it simply demanded that wealth bow to wisdom and serve eternal purposes.

In these pages, my friend *Dr. Bonadie* tackles a daring thesis: *the same God who guided shepherds and kings into unimaginable riches still guides innovators, investors, and philanthropists today.* This book is not a get-rich-quick formula; it is a *get-aligned-forever manifesto.* You will journey from Abraham's covenant fortunes to Solomon's trillion-dollar wisdom, tracing patterns of obedience, generosity, and strategic vision that transcend millennia.

What struck me most is the meticulous effort to convert ancient measures, talents, shekels, bushels, into credible modern valuations. Suddenly, the patriarchs are not distant legends but recognizable CEOs of vast enterprises. Yet every valuation is paired with a principle: *faith before finances, purpose before profit, stewardship before status.*

I recommend you read slowly. Highlight the principles. Pray over the application sections. Then dare to act. *May the Spirit who prospered Joseph amid famine ignite creativity in your crisis; may the courage of David spur you to tackle the giants blocking your cash flow; and may the generosity of Boaz reshape how your company serves people experiencing poverty.*

If you are ready to think bigger about God, money, and mission, turn the page. *Your journey toward righteous riches begins now.*

Dr. Stephen Andrews

Senior Pastor, St. John's Pentecostal House of Restoration

CONTENTS

Dedication _____ III

Acknowledgments _____ IV

Foreword _____ VI

Introduction _____ X

Chapter 1: Abraham: The Billionaire By Covenant _____ 1

Chapter 2: Isaac: The Billionaire Who Prospered In Crisis _____ 11

Chapter 3: *Jacob: Strategic Billionaire Through Innovation* _____ 21

Chapter 4: *The Political Billionaire Through Strategic Planning* __ 31

Chapter 6: *Solomon, History's First Trillionaire* _____ 51

Chapter 7: Job, The Billionaire Who Bounced Back _____ 67

Chapter 8: *Boaz, The Righteous Capitalist* _____ 77

Chapter 9: *The Proverbs 31 Millionaire* _____ 85

Chapter 10: *King Josiah, The Billionaire Reformer* _____ 93

Chapter 11: *The Wise Men, Wealthy Worshippers From The East* __ 99

Chapter 12: *Joseph Of Arimathea, The Hidden Billionaire Who Honored The King* __ 109

Chapter 13: *King Josiah, The Billionaire Reformer* _____ 119

Chapter 14: *Hezekiah, The Guardian Of National Wealth* _____ 127

Chapter 15: *Laban, The Opportunist* _____ 135

Chapter 16: *The Pharaohs Of Egypt: Sovereigns Of Surplus* ___ 143

Estimated Wealth: $1 Trillion _____ 143

Chapter 17: *The Rich Young Ruler: When Wealth Meets A Wounded Will* __ 151

Chapter 18: *Queen Vashti: The Billion-Dollar Boundary* _____ 157

Chapter 19163 *Nebuchadnezzar Ii: The Trillionaire Emperor Of Earthly Glory*_____ 163

Chapter 20: Rahab The Redeemed: From Prostitute To Millionaire Matriarch _____ 171

Chapter 21: The Woman Who Touched The Hem: The Broken Millionaire Who Reached For Wholeness _____ 177

Chapter 22: *Cornelius, God's Rich Marine* _____ 185

Chapter 23: *Simon The Tanner, The Millionaire Host Of Divine Interruptions* _____ 193

Chapter 24: *Mary Of Bethany, The Woman Who Lavished Her Fragrance On Jesus* _ 199

Chapter 25: *Philemon, Millionaire Financier Of Ministry* _____ 205

Chapter 26: *Kingdom Wealth Principles: Building Lasting Prosperity By Heaven's Laws* _____ 211

Chapter 27: *Building Modern Wealth God's Way* _____ 221

Conclusion: The Call Of Kingdom Billionaires _____ 231

Appendices _____ 234

Introduction

Wealth Is Not the Enemy of Righteousness

The Bible is not silent about wealth. In fact, it is one of the most wealth-conscious documents in all of ancient literature. From the silver mines of Solomon to the agricultural empires of the patriarchs, Scripture paints a vivid picture of abundance, often in the hands of men and women whom God deeply trusted. The idea that spirituality must be synonymous with poverty is not only unbiblical. *It is dangerous.*

This book is written to challenge that mindset, to confront the lie that money corrupts, and instead to declare: *it is the love of money that corrupts, but the purpose of money can be divine.*

The characters you are about to meet were not just Sunday school stories. They were empire builders, marketplace moguls, political reformers, strategic negotiators, landowners, international traders, and economic visionaries. These individuals, Abraham, Isaac, Jacob, Joseph, David, Solomon, and others, were not merely blessed spiritually. *They were financially fluent and economically influential.*

If their lives were transposed into today's world, they would not be anonymous worshippers at the back of a church. They would be global philanthropists, CEOs, heads of sovereign wealth funds, or leaders of multibillion-dollar agricultural corporations. *They would be featured in Forbes, but they would tithe in faith. They would sit in boardrooms with bankers and bow in prayer rooms before God.*

Why This Book Now?

We live in an era of extreme economic polarity. On one hand, the rich are getting richer. On the other hand, many believers are being taught that wealth is worldly, carnal, or even evil. This misunderstanding is not just theological. It is crippling. It prevents the righteous from rising into positions of resource stewardship and marketplace dominion, right where the Kingdom needs them most.

Yet the Bible declares, *"It is He who gives you the power to get wealth, that He may establish His covenant"* (Deuteronomy 8:18). That word *power* is not a passive idea. It is a God-given capacity to produce, manage, multiply, and steward resources for generational impact and eternal glory.

In the pages ahead, you will explore:

- *How Abraham built wealth through faith and negotiation*
- *How Joseph used strategic crisis management to control a nation's resources*

- *How Solomon scaled international trade to amass unimaginable riches*

- *Why Boaz's generosity created a generational legacy*

- *And why Jesus warned the rich young ruler, not because he had wealth, but because his wealth had him*

Each chapter provides not only historical and biblical context but also estimated modern equivalents of their wealth, so you can grasp the magnitude of what God entrusted to these individuals. More importantly, you will discover timeless principles, disciplines, habits, and heart postures that will help you steward your own financial journey with purpose and divine insight.

What This Book Is Not

This is not a prosperity gospel manual. It does not promise quick wealth, nor does it suggest that everyone will be a billionaire. What it does offer is a blueprint rooted in Scripture, proven across generations, for those who desire to align their financial lives with kingdom purpose. Whether you are a business owner, a ministry leader, a student, or a servant in the marketplace, *this book will equip you to think biblically about money, legacy, and influence.*

A Call to Kingdom Stewards

We are no longer in a season where the church can afford to ignore economics. *Revival without resources is a vision without legs.* The Great Commission requires funding. The cry of the poor requires intervention. The stewardship of nations requires more than prayer. It requires practical, godly billionaires who can move economies toward justice and righteousness.

Let this book awaken the Abraham in you. Let it stir the Solomon in you. Let it challenge the Laban in you, and strengthen the Joseph in you. *It is time for the righteous to rise in wealth, not for selfish ambition, but for kingdom dominion.*

You were not created to get by barely. You were born to manage overflow.

Welcome to the world of *biblical billionaires*. Let the journey begin.

CHAPTER 1

Abraham: The Billionaire by Covenant

Estimated Wealth: $20 Billion

In the landscape of biblical history, few names echo with as much significance as Abraham. Revered as the father of faith by Jews, Christians, and Muslims alike, Abraham was more than a spiritual patriarch. He was a formidable figure of Wealth, influence, and international impact. While modern readers often focus on his spiritual journey and covenant with God, an equally compelling narrative runs parallel. Abraham was a billionaire by ancient standards, and the story of how he developed his Wealth contains powerful lessons for modern wealth-builders.

A Divine Call to Possession

Abraham's wealth journey began not with a business strategy or inheritance, but with a divine instruction. In *Genesis 12:1-3,* God called Abram (his original name) to leave his country, kindred, and father's house for a land He would show him. This command came with a sevenfold blessing, including land, fame, fruitfulness, and the power to bless others. Abraham's first act of wealth acquisition was obedience. He stepped away from the familiar to embrace the unknown, propelled by a promise.

In the modern world, wealth creation often begins with risk: starting a business, moving to a new market, or leaving a job to pursue a calling. Abraham's story mirrors this truth. He left behind the established prosperity of Ur, a flourishing Mesopotamian city, and became a nomadic entrepreneur led by divine vision. The principle is timeless: *destiny requires departure.* Faith-driven decisions often precede financial fruit.

The Wealth Equation: Obedience + Opportunity

Genesis 13:2 states, *"And Abram was very rich in cattle, in silver, and in gold."* This verse is more than a casual mention. It is a financial profile. Cattle represented portable Wealth and food supply. Silver and gold indicated transactional power and long-term investment. Abraham's portfolio was diversified, resembling a modern billionaire with assets in agriculture, commodities, and real estate.

But how did he get there? *Genesis 12:10–20* describes Abraham's journey into Egypt during a famine. There, Pharaoh bestowed great Wealth upon him, including livestock, silver, gold, and servants, after taking Sarah into his house, believing she was Abraham's sister.

Though the circumstances were ethically complicated, the outcome was an increase in Wealth. Abraham left Egypt far richer than when he entered. This moment reveals another wealth principle: *divine favor can increase Wealth even in foreign, adverse, or ethically ambiguous contexts.*

What we learn here is that obedience opens doors, and doors create opportunity. Abraham was not idle; he traveled, traded, and interacted with kings. He engaged with local economies and respected their systems while leveraging spiritual authority. Faith did not isolate him. It integrated him into commerce and diplomacy.

Strategic Separation Brings Multiplication

As Abraham's flocks and herds grew, so did the conflict with Lot's herdsmen. In *Genesis 13:6-9,* Abraham makes a decisive move. He offers Lot the first choice of the land to prevent strife. Lot chooses the fertile Jordan Valley, while Abraham settles in the less attractive Canaanite hill country. Yet immediately after this separation, God reaffirms and expands Abraham's promise: *"Lift your eyes… all the land you see I will give to you and your offspring forever"* (*Genesis 13:14-15*).

Here lies a critical wealth-building principle: *peaceful separation is often a prerequisite to personal multiplication.* Abraham refused to fight over territory and instead chose faith in God's provision. In return, he gained a prophetic vision of long-term ownership.

Modern entrepreneurs often discover that the key to expansion is letting go of strained partnerships, toxic collaborators, or misaligned priorities. Abraham's humility and generosity in deferring to Lot exemplify the kind of character that sustains Wealth after it is acquired.

War and Wealth: Conquest and Spoils

Genesis 14 tells the story of a dramatic battle in which Abraham leads 318 trained servants to rescue Lot from four allied kings who had conquered Sodom. Not only does Abraham defeat these kings, but he also recovers all the people and possessions they had taken.

This chapter introduces a surprising dimension to Abraham's Wealth: military strategy and conquest. In ancient times, warfare was often tied to economics. Victorious leaders seized cattle, gold, silver, slaves, and land. Abraham, despite being a spiritual man, was also a trained military leader capable of defending his interests and securing assets.

More importantly, this event introduces Melchizedek, king of Salem and priest of God Most High, who blesses Abraham and receives a tithe from him. Abraham's response reveals two major principles:

1. *Tithing is a recognition that Wealth is sourced in the divine.*

2. *Honor releases a higher blessing.*

Abraham could have kept all the spoils for himself. Instead, he tithed and refused to enrich himself through the king of Sodom, saying, *"Lest you should say, 'I have made Abram rich'"* (*Genesis 14:23*). He demonstrated moral clarity in the face of material temptation.

This story shows us that true Wealth is not just measured by what you accumulate, but by how you handle power and position. Abraham was not greedy; he was principled. In our world, billionaires are often admired for what they possess. Abraham is honored for what he refused.

Generational Wealth and Expansion

God's covenant with Abraham deepens in *Genesis 15* and *Genesis 17,* where He promises not just Wealth but generational multiplication. Abraham is told his descendants will be as numerous as the stars and that he will be the *"father of many nations."*

This covenant solidifies the principle of generational Wealth, not just in terms of assets, but in legacy. Abraham's descendants, Isaac, Jacob, Joseph, inherited not only land and livestock but also a promise, a reputation, and a relationship with God.

Today's billionaires often think in terms of family offices, trust funds, and intergenerational investing. Abraham laid the foundation for this thinking thousands of years ago. He did not just build riches; *he built a righteous legacy.* He trained his household in righteousness (*Genesis 18:19*), lived with honor among pagans, and left behind a model of faithful stewardship that spanned centuries.

Estimated Net Worth of Abraham

While we cannot convert ancient Wealth directly into U.S. dollars, we can estimate Abraham's worth based on biblical descriptions and historical economics:

- Cattle, camels, donkeys, and flocks: thousands of heads of livestock

- Silver and gold: likely hundreds of pounds

- Servants and labor force: over 300 trained warriors implies hundreds more in household staff

- Land and water rights: multiple wells and grazing territories in strategic locations

Taken together, a conservative modern estimate of Abraham's net worth could range between **$10 and $20 billion.** In ancient terms, he would be comparable to a regional king or economic governor.

Principles of Wealth from Abraham's Life

Let us consolidate the timeless principles we can learn from Abraham's financial journey:

1. Obey divine instructions, even when they disrupt comfort zones. Wealth often follows obedience, not logic.

2. Go where God sends you, even if you do not have all the details. Vision is progressive; clarity comes with movement.

3. Be generous, even when it seems like you are giving away an advantage. Abraham gave Lot the better land and still received the greater inheritance.

4. Engage in battle, when necessary, but do not compromise your values. Protect your people and possessions with honor.

5. Tithe and give honor where it is due. Financial obedience releases spiritual authority.

6. Pursue legacy, not just liquidity. Built for generations, not indulgence.

7. Separate from toxic relationships peacefully to make room for divine multiplication. Let go of Lot so you can receive Canaan.

8. Trust in God's timeline, not your own panic. Abraham waited decades for Isaac, but the promise stood firm.

9. Reject dishonest gain. Abraham refused Wealth from Sodom's king to maintain spiritual credibility.

10. Model righteousness within your household. Abraham trained his family in justice and uprightness. Wealth and wisdom must co-exist.

Conclusion: A Billionaire by Covenant

Abraham's life is a wealth blueprint that transcends time, culture, and currency. He shows us that Wealth is not inherently sinful, but it must be anchored in obedience, integrity, and purpose. His riches were not for personal indulgence but for covenant establishment.

In a world that celebrates material success but often ignores spiritual responsibility, Abraham stands as a potent reminder: *the wealthiest man is the one who walks with God, gives with honor, fights with purpose, and builds for eternity.*

Your journey toward covenant wealth may not look like Abraham's in geography, but it can mirror his principles in spirit. Like him, you may need to leave your Ur, trust through famine, tithe when it feels risky, and walk by faith into unknown territory. But know this: *when you build on God's covenant, the riches that come will not only sustain you, they will multiply through generations.*

You were never meant to scrape through life. You were designed to inherit nations. Abraham's story is not just history. It is a prototype.

And you, dear reader, are next in line.

"Prosperity is not preserved by inheritance, it is multiplied through obedience and innovation, even in times of famine."

CHAPTER 2

Isaac: The Billionaire Who Prospered in Crisis

Estimated Wealth: $10 Billion

In the grand narrative of Wealth among the patriarchs, Isaac often stands in the shadow of his father Abraham and his son Jacob. Yet his story carries profound financial insight. Isaac didn't just inherit Wealth, he multiplied it in the midst of a national crisis. His life illustrates how obedience, innovation, and persistence in adversity can generate incredible prosperity.

In an age of inflation, market uncertainty, and economic collapse, Isaac's example offers a timeless guide for becoming a billionaire when everyone else is in survival mode.

The Son of a Billionaire

Isaac was born into Wealth. As the promised son of Abraham and Sarah, he grew up under the covering of immense blessing. Abraham's livestock, silver, gold, and servants were transferred to Isaac upon his father's death (*Genesis 25:5*).

But being born into Wealth does not guarantee financial increase. Many heirs squander their inheritance through mismanagement or idleness. Isaac, however, did not coast on his father's accomplishments, he expanded the legacy.

Inheriting Wealth can be a head start or a handicap. The modern equivalent would be a second-generation entrepreneur inheriting a thriving business. Isaac faced the same question many heirs face today: *Will you preserve, or will you produce?* His life answers the question definitively, he became a billionaire not by preservation alone but by production, expansion, and innovation.

The Famine That Tested His Faith

Genesis 26 opens with a scene of economic hardship: *"And there was a famine in the land, beside the first famine that was in the days of Abraham..." (Genesis 26:1)*.

Famine in ancient times meant failed crops, economic slowdown, and migration. Most people fled to Egypt, where food supplies were managed and available. Isaac, following logic, considered this escape. But God interrupted his plan and said, *"Do not go down into Egypt; dwell in the land which I shall tell you of" (Genesis 26:2)*.

This was the beginning of Isaac's test of faith. Would he obey God even when common sense dictated otherwise? Staying in a famine-stricken land made no human sense. But Isaac obeyed the voice of God and remained in Gerar.

Modern application is straightforward: many people abandon purpose for profit, leaving faith zones for comfort zones. Isaac's story teaches that location by divine instruction is more important than location by economic prediction. God's command came with a promise: *"Sojourn in this land, and I will be with you and bless you..."* (*Genesis 26:3*). And indeed, He did.

The Hundredfold Return: Divine Agriculture

One of the most astonishing verses in the Bible appears in *Genesis 26:12*: *"Then Isaac sowed in that land, and received in the same year an hundredfold: and the Lord blessed him."*

In an agrarian society during famine, this was nothing short of miraculous. Sowing seeds into parched soil was risky, even foolish. But Isaac was not investing based on weather patterns, he was investing based on a word from God. His obedience released an agricultural explosion. In a time when others were hungry, Isaac was harvesting.

This verse presents a powerful principle: *don't wait for ideal conditions to act, move on the word you've been given.* Wealth is often built by those who plant when others panic. [1]

While others were hoarding or fleeing, Isaac was sowing. His results were not marginal, they were exponential.

Economists today talk about ROI, Return on Investment. A hundredfold return is equivalent to a 10,000% ROI. In today's agricultural industry, such a return would be considered supernatural. Imagine investing $1 million and receiving $100 million in a year. That is the scale of what Isaac experienced. It positioned him as a dominant economic force in the region.

From Great to Very Great: The Compounding of Wealth

Genesis 26:13 continues: *"And the man waxed great, and went forward, and grew until he became very great."* The original Hebrew conveys ongoing, compounding increase. Isaac's Wealth didn't spike and level off, it expanded progressively over time.

---

[1] *A hundredfold return equals 10,000% ROI, far beyond natural economics. Genesis 26:12–14 shows this was supernatural increase, not market-driven gain.*

Verse 14 explains how: *"For he had possession of flocks, and possession of herds, and a great store of servants: and the Philistines envied him."*

Isaac had diversified assets. He wasn't just an agriculturalist, he was a livestock magnate, a human resource manager, and a landowner. His economic engine had multiple cylinders. In today's terms, he would be running a conglomerate that included farming, meat production, employment services, and perhaps even supply chain infrastructure.

His prosperity was so visible and undeniable that it drew envy and resistance. This brings us to an often-ignored reality: *great Wealth attracts great warfare.* The Philistines responded by stopping up the wells Abraham had dug and driving Isaac away. Prosperity will often provoke opposition, not because you've done wrong, but because your success disrupts others' comfort zones.

Digging Again: Resilience in the Face of Rejection

Isaac's response to opposition is one of the most instructive parts of his story. Instead of fighting for the closed wells or retaliating against the Philistines, he moved on. He reopened old wells and dug new ones. Each time the Philistines quarreled over them, Isaac moved on and dug again.

This sequence of moving, digging, quarreling, and moving again happens multiple times until finally, Isaac digs a well, and no one disputes it. He names it *Rehoboth*, meaning *"broad places"* or *"room,"* saying, *"For now the Lord has made room for us, and we shall be fruitful in the land"* (*Genesis 26:22*).

Isaac teaches us the power of persistence. Every blocked well became a setup for a better opportunity. He did not let setbacks stop him from seeking flow. Wells in the ancient world were not mere conveniences; they were economic lifelines. Control of water meant control of agriculture, livestock, and trade.

Today, a blocked *well* could be a failed investment, a lost business, or a terminated contract. Isaac's story says: *dig again.* Don't war over rejection, work until redirection leads you to expansion.

Covenant and Confirmation

Following the breakthrough at Rehoboth, Isaac goes up to Beersheba, where the Lord appears to him again and reaffirms the covenant: *"Fear not, for I am with thee, and will bless thee, and multiply thy seed for my servant Abraham's sake"* (*Genesis 26:24*).

In response, Isaac builds an altar, pitches his tent, and his servants dig another well. We see here the rhythm of Isaac's life: **altar, tent, and well.**

- **Altar:** Spiritual alignment and divine gratitude

- **Tent:** Flexibility and readiness to move with God

- **Well:** Practical productivity and sustained economic flow

Wealth in the kingdom is not built by chasing trends. It's built by maintaining intimacy with God (*altar*), staying mobile and humble (*tent*), and digging consistently where others quit (*well*).

Estimated Net Worth of Isaac

To understand Isaac's net worth, we must consider the following:

- Inheritance from Abraham: livestock, silver, gold, and many servants

- Hundredfold agricultural return during famine: an unprecedented economic breakthrough

- Possession of many herds and flocks: equivalent to today's large-scale livestock operations

- Control of water rights: in arid regions, equivalent to owning critical infrastructure

- Servants and labor force: hundreds, if not thousands, of workers

Given these factors, Isaac's Wealth in today's valuation could easily exceed $10 billion. Some scholars argue he may have even surpassed Abraham in sheer volume of assets, especially considering his compounding expansion during the crisis.

Lessons from Isaac's Billionaire Journey

Let's extract the wealth principles embedded in Isaac's story:

1. Obey even when logic says flee. The voice of God will consistently outperform market analysts.

2. Sow in scarcity. Those who invest when others withdraw reap when others beg.

3. Measure growth by momentum. Isaac waxed great and kept moving forward. True Wealth builds progressively.

4. Diversify your portfolio. Isaac had agriculture, livestock, labor, and land.

5. Let envy fuel your focus, not your fights. Ignore competitors and keep digging.

6. Don't let rejection define you. Every stopped-up well is an invitation to discover a new stream.

7. Persistence outpaces persecution. Isaac succeeded not by force but by endurance.

8. Worship before you work. Build altars before you build enterprises.

9. Align with generational covenant. Isaac didn't start the promise, but he lived in the benefit of Abraham's covenant.

10. Build for mobility and scalability. Isaac's tent life reminds us not to settle, keep moving as God directs.

Conclusion: Billionaire in a Drought

Isaac's story is a masterclass in resilient Wealth. He prospered not in ideal conditions but in famine. He thrived not because of circumstance but because of covenant. While others withered, he flourished, and he did it with integrity, faith, and remarkable patience.

His life speaks to every entrepreneur, investor, and believer facing a drought today: *You don't need a perfect economy to prosper. You need an explicit instruction, unwavering obedience, and a willingness to dig until the water flows.*

Isaac was not just a custodian of his father's blessing; he was a multiplier of it. His story reminds us that the same God who blessed

Abraham can bless you, even in crisis. When others see a dry land, dig anyway. Your Rehoboth is waiting.

You may not be standing in a fertile valley. But if God told you to stay, to sow, and to dig, get ready. A hundredfold return is still possible.

CHAPTER 3

Jacob: Strategic Billionaire Through Innovation

Estimated Wealth: $20 Billion

Jacob's journey to billionaire status was not born of inheritance but ingenuity. Unlike his grandfather *Abraham*, who God called into covenant wealth, or his father *Isaac*, who reaped a hundredfold return by obedience in famine, Jacob's wealth was built through shrewd negotiation, relentless hard work, and creative problem-solving. His life illustrates how those without a strong financial start can still achieve massive success through persistence, innovation, and strategy.

Born for Legacy, Not Luxury

Jacob was born the second of twins, grasping the heel of his brother *Esau* at birth. This small gesture became symbolic of his life: reaching, contending, and eventually overtaking. Although he was the grandson of *Abraham* and son of *Isaac*, Jacob did not begin his life with access to their wealth. Instead, he lived under the weight of family conflict and the pressure of generational expectation.

Genesis 25:23 records God's prophecy to *Rebekah*: *"Two nations are in thy womb... and the elder shall serve the younger."* From the start, Jacob had a divine assignment. But divine prophecy must be matched with diligent action. His rise to wealth would not come through simple inheritance; it would come through adversity, shrewdness, and spiritual encounters.

The Cost of Deception and the Road to Exile

Jacob's first attempt to shift destiny came through cunning. He traded a bowl of stew for Esau's birthright and later, with *Rebekah's* help, deceived *Isaac* to receive the blessing meant for his brother. These actions, though legally binding in the spiritual realm, triggered a familial crisis. Jacob fled for his life, running not toward opportunity but away from danger. He arrived at his uncle *Laban's* house empty-handed.

This moment marks an essential truth: you don't have to start with wealth to build wealth. Jacob had a prophecy over his life, a blessing in his spirit, and nothing in his pockets. But what he lacked in assets, he made up for in vision and work ethic.

Working with Laban: Strategic Labor

Jacob began working for *Laban* as a servant. He agreed to serve seven years for the right to marry *Rachel*, Laban's younger daughter.

Laban, however, tricked him by giving him *Leah* instead. Jacob ended up working another seven years for *Rachel*.

These 14 years of labor represent Jacob's foundational phase of wealth-building. He worked tirelessly to build a life while accumulating minimal personal wealth. But everything changed in *Genesis 30*. After fulfilling his marriage obligations, Jacob requested compensation for his work.

He proposed a deal: *"Give me every speckled and spotted sheep and every black lamb… and they shall be my wages."* It seemed like an odd and unlikely method to build wealth, but Jacob had a plan.

Laban agreed, thinking he had outwitted Jacob. He even removed the speckled and spotted livestock from the existing flocks to prevent Jacob's success. But Jacob used selective breeding techniques, including placing striped rods in the water troughs during mating, which increased the likelihood of producing speckled and spotted offspring. Through innovation and diligence, Jacob grew extremely wealthy.

Innovation in Animal Husbandry

Jacob's use of selective breeding was centuries ahead of its time. By understanding the biological and environmental conditions under which animals reproduce, Jacob created a genetic strategy that exponentially increased his share of the flocks.

This was not luck, it was insight, trial, and observation. Jacob didn't fight Laban in court or demand restitution. He outsmarted him in the marketplace.

In today's terms, Jacob might be a startup entrepreneur disrupting an industry using data science and biotech while his competitors use traditional methods.

Genesis 30:43 summarizes the outcome: *"And the man increased exceedingly, and had much cattle, and maidservants, and menservants, and camels, and asses."* Jacob moved from a servant to an empire builder.

Navigating Toxic Partnerships

Jacob's success did not go unnoticed. Laban's sons became jealous, and Laban's attitude shifted. It's a familiar pattern: prosperity often breeds envy. When the atmosphere became hostile, Jacob received a word from God instructing him to return to his homeland (*Genesis 31:3*).

Before leaving, he met with his wives and explained how their father had changed his wages ten times and how God had protected and prospered him.

This episode teaches a key wealth principle: recognize when a partnership has reached its expiration date. Jacob was not afraid to walk away from the man who once gave him his start. He left with his wives, children, and massive herds of livestock.

Many modern professionals struggle with the courage to transition. Whether it's a job, a business partner, or a financial arrangement, discernment is required to know when to move on. Jacob left, not in rebellion, but in obedience. He departed with divine backing.

Wealth in the Wilderness

Jacob's journey back to *Canaan* was not easy. He feared facing *Esau*, whom he had wronged. As he approached their meeting, Jacob split his assets into two camps to protect them in case of attack.

This shows a strategic mind: planning for loss while preparing for peace. Before meeting *Esau*, Jacob had a defining moment: an all-night wrestling encounter with an angel.

In *Genesis 32,* Jacob wrestles until daybreak, refusing to let go until he receives a blessing. The angel touches his thigh, changing his walk forever and changing his name from *Jacob* (*"heel-grabber"* or *"trickster"*) to *Israel* (*"one who struggles with God and prevails"*).

This moment was not just spiritual, it was economic. Jacob was being repositioned to manage not just livestock, but legacy. Wrestling with God marked the transition from hustler to patriarch.

Every wealthy man must eventually face the question: Is your prosperity built on manipulation or divine endorsement?

Meeting Esau: Restitution and Maturity

When Jacob finally meets *Esau*, he offers him hundreds of livestock as a gift of peace. The encounter reveals a matured Jacob: a man who no longer takes by trickery but gives by generosity.

This action, though costly, secured peace and reestablished Jacob's integrity. Wealth builders must learn that reconciliation is worth the investment. Jacob was willing to give away part of his fortune to restore a broken relationship. In doing so, he demonstrated a key principle: peace is a form of prosperity.

Building Altars and Managing Inheritance

Upon returning to *Canaan*, Jacob built an altar in *Shechem* and later moved to *Bethel*, where God reappeared to him. These acts of worship underscore Jacob's growth.

Like his grandfather *Abraham* and his father *Isaac*, Jacob understood that wealth is not secure without spiritual alignment.

Jacob's final years were spent managing his large family, distributing blessings, and setting up his sons for future influence. *Joseph*, his son by *Rachel*, would rise to become a ruler in *Egypt*. *Judah* would become the line through which kings and the Messiah would come.

Even on his deathbed, Jacob was organizing his legacy. His prophetic blessings over his sons in *Genesis 49* are more than poetic, they are visionary. He was distributing inheritance, recognizing gifts, and releasing destiny. An actual billionaire prepares the next generation to expand what he began.

Estimated Net Worth of Jacob

Jacob's wealth is recorded in terms of livestock, servants, and movable assets:

- Flocks of sheep and goats, camels, and donkeys
- A large staff of male and female servants
- Strategic land usage and water rights
- Control over multiple family units and future tribes

Considering his holdings and the economic structures of his time, Jacob's modern equivalent would likely be valued at *$10–15 billion,* comparable to a livestock empire or vertically integrated agricultural company. His wealth was self-made, developed over 20 years in hostile conditions, and rooted in strategy, innovation, and divine intervention.

Wealth Principles from Jacob's Life

1. Start with vision, not wealth. Jacob had a promise before he had possessions.

2. Work diligently, even under unfair conditions. He served faithfully despite Laban's manipulations.

3. Negotiate creatively. His spotted and speckled deal was unconventional but strategic.

4. Innovate with what you have. Jacob used natural resources to influence animal genetics.

5. Leave when it's time. He exited toxic partnerships without burning bridges.

6. Prepare for adversity. Jacob split his camp and prayed before confronting Esau.

7. Wrestle with God for clarity. Your breakthrough often comes after struggle.

8. Prioritize peace. Jacob gave generously to restore his relationship with Esau.

9. Align wealth with worship. He built altars before building empires.

10. Think in generations. Jacob's wealth wasn't just personal, it was tribal and prophetic.

Conclusion: The Innovator's Wealth

Jacob's story is not a tale of quick riches but of strategic growth. He demonstrates that innovation, resilience, and negotiation can generate immense wealth even when starting with nothing.

He teaches us that God blesses ingenuity when it is wrapped in integrity. And perhaps most powerfully, he shows that every struggle carries the seed of transformation.

In a world full of imitators, Jacob invites you to be an innovator. In an economy of compromise, he models perseverance. And in the pursuit of legacy, he proves that wrestling with God always leads to a new name and new territory.

You may not be born into wealth. You may have a complicated family history or be working under a *Laban*. But like Jacob, if you keep working, keep believing, and keep strategizing, you can move from a dreamer in exile to a billionaire with influence.

And the best part? What you build won't just bless you, it will shape nations.

CHAPTER 4

Joseph: The Political Billionaire Through Strategic Planning

Estimated Wealth: $500 Billion

Joseph's journey from the pit to the palace is one of the most dramatic and inspiring stories in the Bible. He represents the kind of wealth that doesn't come from inheritance or labor alone, but through strategic leadership, crisis management, and divine favor in high places.

Unlike *Abraham, Isaac,* or *Jacob,* who built wealth through land and livestock, Joseph built wealth by managing systems, solving problems, and administering national resources. He stands as a timeless model of how God can raise a person from obscurity to become a steward of global wealth.

The Seed of Greatness

Joseph was the eleventh son of *Jacob* and the firstborn of *Rachel,* the woman Jacob truly loved. From birth, Joseph carried the weight of divine favor.

Genesis 37 tells us that Joseph was highly favored by his father, which made him a target of his brothers' jealousy. His prophetic dreams, symbols of rulership and elevation, fueled the animosity.

These dreams were not just childish visions; they were early indicators of a divine plan for national influence and economic authority.

Joseph's story begins with favor and quickly shifts to betrayal. His brothers, threatened by his dreams and favored status, sold him into slavery. What seemed like a detour was actually the first step in Joseph's divine elevation.

This highlights a critical truth: the path to the palace often begins in a pit.

From Slave to Steward

Joseph was sold to *Potiphar*, an officer of *Pharaoh*, where he excelled as a servant. *Genesis 39:2* says, *"The Lord was with Joseph, and he became a successful man."*

Joseph's success wasn't tied to his environment but to God's presence. He managed Potiphar's entire household with excellence and integrity.

This season of his life reveals a powerful principle: prosperity is not where you are, it's who you are. Joseph didn't wait for a title to act with excellence. He managed another man's house as if it were his own, that kind of stewardship positions a person for promotion.

Faithfulness in little always precedes rulership over much. Even when falsely accused by Potiphar's wife and thrown into prison, Joseph maintained his diligence. In prison, he was again elevated to a position of responsibility. The warden entrusted him with the care of all the inmates.

These trials weren't delays; they were leadership laboratories.

Problem-Solving as a Pathway to Promotion

Joseph's rise to power was sealed by his ability to solve problems. In *Genesis 40,* he interprets the dreams of Pharaoh's imprisoned cupbearer and baker.

Two years later, when Pharaoh is troubled by a dream, the cupbearer remembers Joseph. Brought before Pharaoh, Joseph interprets the dream of seven years of plenty followed by seven years of famine.

But he doesn't stop at interpretation, he proposes a national strategy for food storage and economic survival. His plan includes tax collection (one-fifth of the harvest), storage in regional cities, and a centralized administration of resources.

Pharaoh is so impressed that he promotes Joseph to second-in-command over Egypt.

Joseph's genius wasn't just in interpreting dreams, but in designing systems. He implemented what today would be called a national supply chain management system, logistical infrastructure, and a centralized food reserve.

In a time of impending crisis, Joseph offered solutions that not only saved Egypt but also enriched it.

Managing Crisis, Multiplying Wealth

During the seven years of plenty, Joseph oversaw the collection of grain and other food supplies. *Genesis 41:49* says he stored up grain *"like the sand of the sea, very much, until he stopped counting, for it was beyond measure."*

When the famine hit, Joseph didn't just open the storehouses, he implemented an economic strategy that gradually transferred wealth and power to Pharaoh:

1. The people bought grain with money.

2. When the money ran out, they traded livestock.

3. When the livestock was gone, they traded land.

4. Eventually, the people themselves became indentured to Pharaoh in exchange for survival.

By the end of the crisis, Pharaoh controlled nearly all the land, livestock, and labor in Egypt. Joseph, as the architect of this economic empire, managed an operation equivalent to a national treasury, agricultural conglomerate, and internal revenue service.

The Estimated Wealth Managed by Joseph

Though Joseph himself may not have held private ownership of these assets, the wealth he controlled and administered places him firmly among the great economic stewards of all time.

To estimate the scale of what Joseph managed:

- Seven years of complete national harvest stored and preserved

- All financial transactions during the famine

- National livestock industry

- Land acquisitions across Egypt

- Government labor systems

Modern economists could equate his management to overseeing a national GDP worth hundreds of billions, if not more.

He transformed Egypt into a centralized, state-owned enterprise and made Pharaoh the wealthiest ruler on earth at that time.

While Joseph did not own the assets in the way modern billionaires do, he controlled and directed them with absolute authority. His personal compensation, status, marriage into nobility, and freedom to govern placed him at the equivalent of a multi-billionaire-level executive with global influence.

Family Restoration and Wealth Distribution

Joseph's story is not only about managing national wealth but also about restoring family legacy.

When his brothers came to Egypt seeking food, Joseph recognized them but concealed his identity. Over time, he tested their integrity, wept in private, and finally revealed himself in a moment of emotional breakthrough.

Rather than seek revenge, Joseph welcomed his family and relocated them to *Goshen,* the most fertile region in Egypt. He provided for them, established a new home for the nation of Israel, and reconnected with his aging father *Jacob.*

Here we see a beautiful merging of wealth and reconciliation. Joseph used his political and economic power to preserve his lineage. His success wasn't selfish, it was redemptive. His wealth created a refuge for an entire people.

Lessons from Joseph's Billionaire Blueprint

Joseph's life offers profound wealth-building principles:

1. Dream big, but prepare for betrayal. Great dreams often provoke opposition. Don't let betrayal cancel your destiny.

2. Excel in obscurity. Serve faithfully in prison, and God will promote you in the palace.

3. Be a problem-solver. Wealth flows to those who solve real problems in times of crisis.

4. Offer solutions, not just insights. Joseph didn't just interpret dreams, he offered strategies.

5. Create systems, not just short-term fixes. Joseph's economic plan sustained an entire nation.

6. Operate with integrity at every level. Joseph maintained character, even when falsely accused.

7. Don't abuse your power. Joseph could have crushed his brothers, but he chose reconciliation.

8. Align your success with God's purpose. Joseph recognized that his elevation was not about status but about salvation.

9. Leave a legacy beyond riches. Joseph's administration paved the way for Israel's preservation and multiplication.

10. Stay humble in success. Joseph always acknowledged God as the source of his insight and favor.

Conclusion: God's Economist

Joseph stands as a unique figure among biblical billionaires. He did not start with wealth. He did not inherit it. He built influence through faithful service, strategic thinking, and supernatural insight.

He became Pharaoh's right hand, stewarded unimaginable wealth, and reshaped the economy of one of the world's greatest empires. But his most incredible legacy wasn't the grain he stored or the gold he handled, it was the people he saved.

His wealth was a means to a mission. His elevation was a platform for purpose. In a world where billionaires often hoard for vanity, Joseph models stewardship over selfishness. He proves that God can anoint someone to operate at the highest levels of government and business without compromising spiritual integrity.

Today, Joseph's story challenges us: Will we manage the resources God entrusts us with for His glory? Will we rise in adversity, lead with wisdom, and serve with humility?

If you feel forgotten, falsely accused, or stuck in a season of obscurity, take heart. Joseph was once there, too. But he held onto his dream, sharpened his skills, and trusted God's timing. And when the moment came, he was ready to manage a nation.

"True kingship is not measured by crowns or conquests, but by a heart that turns wealth into worship and power into service."

CHAPTER 5

David: The Warrior King with A Billionaire's Heart

Estimated Wealth: $100 Billion

King David is one of the most celebrated figures in Scripture, not just for his spiritual depth and poetic genius, but for his leadership, military conquest, and extraordinary wealth. He was not born into royalty or raised in a palace. He was a shepherd boy, the youngest in his family, overlooked and underestimated. And yet, he rose to become a billionaire king and established the most powerful and prosperous dynasty in ancient Israel. What set David apart was not merely his ability to acquire wealth, but the heart with which he managed it, a heart after God's own.

From Shepherd to Statesman

David's rise to prominence begins in *1 Samuel 16* when the prophet Samuel, under God's instruction, anoints him as king while Saul is still on the throne. This divine appointment would unfold gradually, marked by years of waiting, battles, betrayals, and spiritual refinement.

Though David was not initially enthroned, he began to walk in royal character long before he wore a crown. His journey started in the fields, tending sheep, a job considered lowly. Yet it was there he learned courage (defending his flock from lions and bears), leadership, and intimacy with God.

The principle is clear: wealth and promotion often find those who are faithful in obscurity.

David was later summoned to play music for King Saul, then to serve as his armor-bearer. His defining moment came when he defeated Goliath, not for riches or fame, but because he couldn't tolerate the defiance of God's people. His first reward was not money, but access. He entered royal circles and became part of the king's household.

Strategic Acumen and Military Genius

David's economic influence grew through a series of strategic military victories. As a warrior, he was unmatched. His campaigns against the Philistines, Amalekites, Moabites, Edomites, and others brought both safety and resources into Israel.

In *2 Samuel 8:6* and *8:14*, we read repeatedly that *"the Lord gave David victory wherever he went."* But victory wasn't merely spiritual, it was financial.

Ancient warfare often included seizing the spoils of war, gold, silver, livestock, and even human labor. David understood this and utilized war as an economic strategy to expand national wealth and secure Israel's dominance. He collected treasures from conquered nations and placed them in treasuries dedicated to the Lord.

His military campaigns significantly increased the nation's treasury and his personal royal wealth. In today's terms, David would be a head of state who also served as a five-star general, overseeing national defense, economic expansion through conquest, and foreign diplomacy. His exploits made Israel a military and economic powerhouse.

Wise Alliances and Loyal Men

David didn't accumulate wealth alone. His success was built on his ability to lead and inspire others. The *Mighty Men of David*, a group of elite warriors, demonstrated uncommon loyalty and valor. David inspired such devotion that these men risked their lives to get him water from Bethlehem (*2 Samuel 23:15–17*).

His leadership transformed outcasts into captains and vagabonds into valiant men. Beyond military alliances, David also knew how to foster political relationships. He maintained treaties, respected boundaries with friendly nations, and formed advantageous marriages (though his polygamy brought consequences).

His relationships opened channels for trade, intelligence, and economic cooperation. Modern leaders who build sustainable wealth do so by surrounding themselves with skilled, loyal, and empowered individuals. David's inner circle wasn't just competent, it was covenantal.

Wealth Management for Worship

Perhaps the most stunning expression of David's heart for God, and his use of wealth, is found in *1 Chronicles 29*. Near the end of his life, David began preparing for the building of the temple, which his son Solomon would oversee. Though David was not permitted to build it himself (because he had shed much blood), he gave an unprecedented amount of his personal fortune to fund the project.

1 Chronicles 29:3 records that David donated *"three thousand talents of gold and seven thousand talents of refined silver"* from his personal treasury for the house of God. Scholars estimate that just the gold given by David would be worth over $5–6 billion in today's currency.

Then he turned to the leaders of Israel and asked, *"Now who is willing to consecrate himself today to the Lord?"* Inspired by his generosity, the leaders followed suit and gave massive offerings of gold, silver, bronze, and iron.

This act of radical giving did not deplete David's wealth; it multiplied his influence and solidified his legacy. David understood something that modern billionaires often miss: the highest use of wealth is worship. His giving was not transactional, it was sacrificial. He gave from a place of covenant, not convenience. And in doing so, he established a principle for generations: that true kings give their best to God.

Infrastructure, Trade, and Economic Growth

Under David's reign, Israel expanded its territory and developed its infrastructure. He captured Jerusalem and made it the political and spiritual capital of the nation. He brought the Ark of the Covenant to Jerusalem, effectively unifying national identity, worship, and governance.

David also laid the foundations for Israel's economic expansion. He organized the Levites, established administrative systems, and delegated responsibilities to officers, commanders, scribes, and treasurers. In *1 Chronicles 27–28*, we see an entire structure of civil and military administration designed to support both governance and commerce.

Trade routes were secured, fortresses were built, and agriculture was strengthened. David's reign brought stability, and stability fosters economic growth. In the modern context, David's strategies resemble those of nation-builders and economic reformers who stabilize nations for generational advancement.

The Estimated Wealth of David

David's wealth came from multiple streams:

- **Spoils of war:** Numerous nations were conquered and their treasures brought to Israel.

- **Personal assets:** David had his own treasury from years of leadership and gifts.

- **Voluntary tributes:** Neighboring kings paid homage and gave precious gifts.

- **National treasury:** He managed state income, offerings, and taxation.

Conservatively, David's personal wealth, especially as revealed in his temple donation, could be estimated in modern terms at $10–20 billion, with the national assets he controlled exceeding that figure. However, his true wealth was not measured in gold but in influence, legacy, and worship.

Wealth Principles from David's Life

1. Serve faithfully in obscurity. David served in the pasture before he sat on the throne. Humility precedes promotion.

2. Use your talents to gain access. His music brought him into royal spaces long before he became king.

3. Be willing to fight battles others fear. Slaying Goliath brought recognition, but more importantly, revealed courage.

4. Surround yourself with covenantal alliances. David's Mighty Men and advisors were part of his wealth system.

5. Honor God with your wealth. David gave from his personal treasury to build God's house.

6. Lead with generosity. His giving provoked national giving and unity.

7. Use power to empower others. David raised leaders from obscurity and multiplied influence.

8. Manage resources wisely. He appointed officials to oversee treasuries, agriculture, commerce, and defense.

9. Leave wealth for worship, not just inheritance. His focus was on building a dwelling place for God, not hoarding assets.

10. View wealth as a platform for purpose. Every decision David made aligned with his call to shepherd God's people.

A King After God's Own Heart

What makes David stand out among biblical billionaires is not just the size of his treasury, but the shape of his heart. He wasn't perfect, his moral failures with Bathsheba and Uriah brought consequences, but even in failure, he was quick to repent and return to God.

David's wealth was a reflection of his spiritual posture. He loved God more than gold. He ruled with passion, led with conviction, and gave with abandon. His life speaks to modern leaders, entrepreneurs, and policymakers: wealth without worship is hollow, and power without purpose is dangerous.

His legacy is not merely in silver and gold, but in psalms that stir the soul, a dynasty that brought forth the Messiah, and a heart that gave everything to God.

Conclusion: Billionaire with a Shepherd's Heart

David began with a staff and a sling. He ended with a crown and a kingdom. His story proves that wealth built on worship, leadership, and sacrifice is wealth that endures.

He was a warrior, a poet, a king, and a billionaire, but more than that, he was a man after God's own heart.

In a world where wealth is often pursued without wisdom, David shows us a better way. He reminds us that true kings don't just gather riches, they gather courage, character, and covenant.

Let David's life challenge you: be bold in battle, faithful in obscurity, generous in victory, and humble in glory. Because in the end, the greatest treasure isn't what you store in vaults, but what you sow into eternity.

"When wisdom becomes your greatest pursuit, wealth and honor will follow as God's reward."

CHAPTER 6

Solomon, History's First Trillionaire

Estimated Wealth: $2–3 trillion

Among all the billionaires of the Bible, none compares to the staggering wealth, global fame, and profound wisdom of King Solomon. The son of David and Bathsheba, Solomon inherited a kingdom already strong and stable, but under his rule, Israel reached the pinnacle of economic, political, and cultural influence. Unlike his father, David, whose reign was marked by war, Solomon's reign was characterized by peace and prosperity. He was not only a king, but also a merchant, a builder, a judge, and an international diplomat. Adjusted to modern values, Solomon's wealth positions him as arguably the first trillionaire in human history.

A Young King with a Wise Heart

Solomon's journey to wealth began not with a strategy for riches but with a prayer for wisdom. When God appeared to him in a dream at Gibeon and offered him anything he desired, Solomon's request was profound: *"Give your servant an understanding heart to judge your

²people" (1 Kings 3:9). He asked for wisdom, not wealth, and in doing so received both. God responded, *"Because you have asked this thing... I have also given you what you did not ask, both riches and honor"* (1 Kings 3:11-13).

This moment set the foundation for Solomon's empire. *Wisdom is wealth's most excellent companion.* It is no coincidence that the wealthiest man in the Bible was also the wisest. Solomon teaches us that intellectual capital precedes financial capital. Wealth built without wisdom collapses; wisdom attracts, multiplies, and preserves wealth.

Inheriting Wealth and Building More

Solomon began his reign with access to the vast resources accumulated by his father, David. David had conquered surrounding nations and stored massive quantities of gold, silver, bronze, and other treasures. But Solomon did not merely manage what his father left; he expanded it exponentially.

He forged strategic political marriages, most notably with Pharaoh's daughter, and entered trade agreements with nations as far away as India, Arabia, and North Africa. He partnered with Hiram, king of

---

[2] Solomon inherited David's wealth but multiplied it through trade, alliances, and innovation. His annual 666 talents of gold (1 Kings 10:14) equal roughly 25 tons, over $1.2 billion today.

Tyre, to build ships and import valuable goods. Under Solomon's leadership, Israel became a global trade hub, with gold, silver, spices, exotic animals, ivory, and fine wood flowing into the land.

The Gold Standard: Literal and Figurative

1 Kings 10:14 reports: *"The weight of gold that came to Solomon in one year was six hundred threescore and six talents of gold."* That's 666 talents, or approximately 25 tons of gold annually. In modern terms, this equals over **$1.2 billion per year in gold alone**, not counting other revenue streams.

But Solomon's wealth extended far beyond gold:

- **Customs and taxation**: Foreign merchants paid tribute for access to Israel's thriving markets.

- **Imports and exports**: Solomon controlled international trade routes, especially along the Red Sea.

- **Military monopoly**: He supplied horses and chariots to surrounding nations at a profit (1 Kings 10:28–29).

- **Tributes and gifts**: Kings and queens brought wealth in exchange for Solomon's counsel and alliances.

When the Queen of Sheba visited to test Solomon's wisdom, she brought *"120 talents of gold, large quantities of spices, and precious stones"* (1 Kings 10:10). Solomon's wisdom had monetary value; his reputation itself generated income.

The Temple and the Palace: Building with Grandeur

One of Solomon's greatest legacies was the construction of the temple in Jerusalem. Envisioned initially by David, it became Solomon's crowning architectural and spiritual achievement. Built with cedar from Lebanon, pure gold overlays, bronze furnishings, and precious stones, it was a wonder of its time.

Beyond the temple, Solomon built his palace, administrative buildings, fortified cities, and military installations. These projects weren't merely functional; they were luxurious. Modern estimates suggest that Solomon's temple alone would cost billions to replicate today. His infrastructure investments not only honored God but also created jobs, unified the kingdom, and attracted global admiration.

National Prosperity: Israel's Golden Age

During Solomon's reign, prosperity was widespread. 1 Kings 4:20 records: *"Judah and Israel were as numerous as the sand by the sea... eating and drinking and rejoicing."* Later, 1 Kings 10:27 adds: *"The king made silver as common in Jerusalem as stones."*

This is staggering. Silver, once a precious metal, became commonplace. Solomon elevated the economy so much that abundance touched every household. His administration was not exploitative; it was expansive. He created systems that distributed wealth, stabilized the economy, and uplifted the ordinary citizen.

Estimated Net Worth of Solomon

Calculating Solomon's net worth involves combining several streams:

- Annual gold revenue: **$1.2 billion+**

- Trade and imports: vast but unquantified

- Tributes and taxes: likely billions more

- Infrastructure and cities: extensive holdings

- Agriculture and livestock: large-scale operations

- Natural resources: forests, mines, and waterways

Conservative estimates place Solomon's modern equivalent wealth between **$2–3 trillion**, making him arguably the wealthiest man who ever lived. His kingdom functioned as a financial empire, driven by wisdom, strategy, and divine alignment.

Decline Through Excess

Despite his astronomical success, Solomon's life also teaches the danger of excess. In his later years, he amassed 700 wives and 300 concubines, many from foreign nations, who turned his heart toward their gods. 1 Kings 11:4 records: *"His heart was not loyal to the Lord his God, as was the heart of his father David."*

This spiritual drift led Solomon to tolerate idol worship, build altars to pagan gods, and compromise his integrity. As a result, God declared that the kingdom would be divided after his death, a tragic consequence of divided loyalties.

The lesson is sobering: *wealth without worship eventually decays.* Solomon had everything, power, pleasure, prestige, but lost the purity of devotion that had once made him great.

Solomon, History's First Trillionaire (Revised with Wealth-Building Proverbs)

Among the billionaires of the Bible, no one rivals the staggering opulence and wisdom of King Solomon.

His wealth was so immense, his wisdom so profound, and his influence so far-reaching that historians and economists alike consider him the first trillionaire in human history. Yet Solomon's story is not just about material gain; it's about the divine wisdom that makes wealth sustainable, ethical, and impactful.

Solomon's prosperity was rooted not in ambition, but in alignment with divine purpose. He didn't ask God for money, armies, or fame. Instead, he asked for wisdom, and everything else followed.

A Prayer for Wisdom That Brought Wealth

Solomon's rise began with a defining moment. In 1 Kings 3, God appeared to him in a dream and offered him a blank check:

"Ask what I shall give thee."

Solomon humbly requested a discerning heart to govern the people.

Pleased with the request, God promised him not only wisdom but also *"riches and honor like no king before or after you."*

This decision demonstrates a timeless truth: *wisdom is the most profitable investment a person can make.* Solomon later echoed this principle in Proverbs 3:13-14:

"Blessed is the one who finds wisdom… for she is more profitable than silver and yields better returns than gold."

Proverbs Wealth-Building Lesson #1

"Wisdom is the foundation of wealth" (Proverbs 4:7).

"Wisdom is the principal thing; therefore, get wisdom." Before money multiplies, the mind must mature.

Inheritance, Trade, and Global Diplomacy

Solomon inherited a unified and wealthy kingdom from his father, David, but he didn't stop there. He expanded it through trade agreements, international alliances, and large-scale construction. He established shipping fleets with Hiram of Tire, brought in gold from Ophir, spices from Arabia, and rare animals from distant lands. Through taxation, customs duties, and tributes, Solomon turned Israel into a commercial superpower.

Proverbs Wealth-Building Lesson #2

"Hard work produces wealth; laziness leads to poverty" (Proverbs 10:4).

"He becomes poor who deals with a slack hand, but the hand of the diligent makes rich."

Solomon didn't just work hard himself; he empowered an entire administration of diligent officers and managers.

Gold by the Ton

1 Kings 10:14 states that Solomon received 666 talents of gold annually, about 25 tons.

This equals over **$1.2 billion per year in modern terms.** But this was just the beginning. He also received goods from traders, tributes from rulers, and revenues from business ventures.

Proverbs Wealth-Building Lesson #3

"Multiple streams of income protect against loss" (Proverbs 27:23–27).

Solomon's income came from agriculture, mining, import-export trade, military logistics, and royal patronage.

Building the Temple and National Infrastructure

Solomon's construction of the temple was both a spiritual and economic feat. Using the finest cedar, gold, bronze, and marble, he erected a structure that became the central symbol of Israel's covenant with God.

Beyond the temple, he built palaces, cities, storehouses, and ports. This productivity created jobs and strengthened national identity.

Proverbs Wealth-Building Lesson #4

"Wealth comes through wise planning and diligent labor" (Proverbs 21:5).

"The plans of the diligent lead to profit as surely as haste leads to poverty."

Wealth Distribution and National Prosperity

Under Solomon, wealth wasn't hoarded, it was shared. 1 Kings 4:20 says, *"Judah and Israel were many... eating and drinking and making merry."* Later, 1 Kings 10:27 adds, *"The king made silver as common in Jerusalem as stones."*

This prosperity was no accident. Solomon governed with both fiscal intelligence and social awareness.

Proverbs Wealth-Building Lesson #5

"Wise rulers build wealth for others" (Proverbs 29:4).

"By justice, a king gives a country stability, but those who are greedy for bribes tear it down."

The Wealth of a Trillionaire

Modern economists estimate Solomon's net worth, including revenues, precious metals, international trade, and real estate, at **$2–3 trillion**, surpassing today's wealthiest magnates.

Proverbs Wealth-Building Lesson #6

"Wise speech leads to favor and opportunity" (Proverbs 13:2; 22:11).

Solomon's wisdom drew leaders who gladly paid to hear him speak.

Proverbs Wealth-Building Lesson #7

"A good reputation is more desirable than riches" (Proverbs 22:1).

Solomon's name was his brand, sought out by rulers across the world.

Proverbs Wealth-Building Lesson #8

"Honor the Lord with your wealth" (Proverbs 3:9-10).

Solomon honored God with the first fruits of his increase, primarily through the temple.

Proverbs Wealth-Building Lesson #9

"The generous will prosper" (Proverbs 11:25).

Solomon gave freely to God and others, ensuring favor and flow.

Proverbs Wealth-Building Lesson #10

"A fool and his money are soon parted" (Proverbs 21:20).

Solomon warned against wasteful living; his wisdom safeguarded the nation's wealth.

The Danger of Drift

Despite his divine wisdom and historic wealth, Solomon's heart eventually drifted. He married foreign wives who brought their gods into Israel. By the end of his reign, idolatry weakened the nation's spiritual foundation.

Proverbs Wealth-Building Lesson #11

"Guard your heart" (Proverbs 4:23).

"For out of it are the issues of life." Wealth without integrity leads to collapse.

Proverbs Wealth-Building Lesson #12

"Don't be enslaved by your appetites" (Proverbs 23:1–3).

Solomon himself warned of indulgence, though his later years reflected these missteps.

Proverbs Wealth-Building Lesson #13

"Don't envy oppressors or take shortcuts to riches" (Proverbs 28:6, 22).

Solomon built ethically; his decline came when he tolerated compromise.

Proverbs Wealth-Building Lesson #14

"Wealth gained hastily will dwindle" (Proverbs 13:11).

The prosperity of his heirs quickly faded because they failed to walk in wisdom.

Proverbs Wealth-Building Lesson #15

"The fear of the Lord is the beginning of wisdom" (Proverbs 9:10).

This was the anchor Solomon abandoned, and the lesson we must retain.

Final Reflections: Wealth, Wisdom, and Worship

Solomon's life is both an inspiration and a cautionary tale. He teaches us that wealth is a byproduct of wisdom, that systems multiply prosperity, and that God honors leaders who steward resources faithfully. But he also warns us that spiritual drift, moral compromise, and unchecked appetites can undo even the most excellent fortune.

His Proverbs remain one of the most potent collections of financial, ethical, and relational wisdom the world has ever known. They echo across cultures, boardrooms, banks, and pulpits.

Conclusion: The Legacy of Solomon

Solomon was not just a king; he was a kingdom architect, an economic pioneer, and a prophet of prosperity principles. His reign shows what is possible when divine wisdom governs wealth.

His story challenges us to pursue not just riches, but righteous riches, prosperity that honors God, serves people, and endures for generations.

You don't have to be born in a palace to learn from Solomon. Read his Proverbs. Apply them daily. Build wisely. Give generously. Rule your world with wisdom.

And never forget: *true wealth begins in the heart, is governed by wisdom, and is fulfilled in worship.*

"True wealth is not measured by what you keep in times of plenty, but by what remains unshaken when everything is stripped away."

CHAPTER 7

Job, The Billionaire Who Bounced Back

Estimated Wealth: $20 Billion

Job's story is unlike any other in the biblical narrative of wealth. He is known not just for his fortune but for his faith during affliction and resilience in restoration. If Solomon shows us how to acquire wealth through wisdom, and David reveals how to conquer it through warfare, Job teaches us how to survive when it all collapses, and how to recover stronger.

Job was a man of integrity, affluence, and profound spiritual awareness. The book that bears his name opens not with a birth or coronation, but with an introduction highlighting both his righteousness and his riches: *"There was a man in the land of Uz, whose name was Job; and that man was perfect and upright, and one that feared God, and eschewed evil"* (Job 1:1).

A Man of Wealth and Worship

Job wasn't just righteous, he was wealthy. *Job 1:3* describes his estate: *"His substance also was seven thousand sheep, and three thousand camels, and five hundred yokes of oxen, and five hundred she-asses, and a very great household."* The text concludes, *"so that this man was the greatest of all the men of the east."*

This confirms that Job was the wealthiest man in his region. His portfolio was based on large-scale agricultural and livestock operations, which in the ancient world made him equivalent to a billionaire farmer-industrialist. His wealth wasn't speculative, it was tangible and labor-intensive, involving land, water rights, servants, and trade.

Job also had ten children, whom he raised with intentionality. He offered sacrifices for them regularly, just in case they had *"cursed God in their hearts."* His wealth did not distract him from spiritual duty; it motivated more profound devotion.

The Wealth-Building Structure of Job's Life

Job's prosperity came from several identifiable systems:

- Livestock multiplication: sheep, camels, oxen, and donkeys for wool, transportation, farming, and trade

- Large staff: *"a very great household"* implies he employed hundreds, perhaps thousands

- Land holdings: to sustain this many animals, he must have owned vast tracts of pastureland

- Reputation: Job was not only wealthy, but he was also influential. Others sought his counsel and honored his leadership.

Though we lack exact numbers, if we estimate Job's holdings in today's value, a conservative estimate would place him easily within the multi-billion-dollar range, possibly $10 billion or more. He would be comparable to a Jeff Bezos of the ancient agricultural economy, diverse, dominant, and respected.

When the Bottom Falls Out

In one of the most harrowing turns in biblical literature, Job loses everything. One messenger after another arrives with devastating news: his livestock are stolen or destroyed, his servants are slaughtered, and his children are killed in a windstorm. Then, as if external loss weren't enough, Job is struck with painful boils from head to toe.

Despite this unimaginable suffering, Job does something extraordinary. He worships: *"Naked I came from my mother's womb, and naked I shall return; the Lord gave, and the Lord hath taken away; blessed be the name of the Lord"* (Job 1:21).

This reveals Job's true wealth: a heart tethered to God, not to gold. He teaches us that the most significant test of prosperity is not how much you gain, but how you respond when you lose it.

Spiritual Warfare Lessons

Job's wealth was grounded in agricultural empire-building, human resources, and logistics. Yet, despite his riches, he led his family in prayer and consecration, offering sacrifices daily, anticipating spiritual risk.

- **Spiritual Warfare Lesson #1:** Wealth does not exempt you from spiritual attack, it often attracts it. Satan targets influential people who steward wealth righteously because of their generational impact.

Job's diligence in prayer was not paranoia; it was prophetic defense. He knew spiritual realities affect natural outcomes.

The Spiritual Battle Behind the Scenes

What Job didn't know, but the reader is told, is that a heavenly conversation had taken place. In *Job 1:6-12*, Satan presents himself before God and accuses Job, claiming he only serves God because of blessings. God permits Satan to test Job, stripping him of possessions and children, but not his life.

- **Spiritual Warfare Lesson #2:** Sometimes you're under attack because of how right you are, not how wrong. Job's trials were not punishment but proof of God's confidence in his integrity.

- **Spiritual Warfare Lesson #3:** The enemy uses accusations to open doors of affliction. *Revelation 12:10* calls Satan *"the accuser of the brethren."* His weapon is words, and his access is often permitted through divine purpose, not demonic power alone.

- **Spiritual Warfare Lesson #4:** The battlefield may be invisible, but the results are tangible. Loss, sickness, and betrayal in Job's life were physical symptoms of a spiritual conflict.

The Loyalty of God Over the Logic of Men

Throughout Job's trials, his friends Eliphaz, Bildad, and Zophar argued that his suffering must be due to sin. They equated loss with guilt and prosperity with righteousness. But Job refused to confess to something he had not done. He held fast to his integrity, even as he wrestled with God.

This was Job's ultimate wealth test: character. Stripped of all material status and reduced to a man sitting in ashes, scraping his sores, Job still spoke faith-filled words:

- *"Though He slay me, yet will I trust Him"* (Job 13:15)

- *"I know that my Redeemer lived..."* (Job 19:25)

The Restoration of the Righteous

Job 42 records the turning point. God speaks, rebukes Job's friends, and restores Job's fortunes. Verse 10 declares: *"And the Lord turned the captivity of Job, when he prayed for his friends: also, the Lord gave Job twice as much as he had before."*

This principle is profound: healing begins when you pray for those who misunderstood you. Job's restoration was not triggered by money or labor, but by intercession. He forgave, he prayed, and God multiplied.

Verse 12 continues: *"So the Lord blessed the latter end of Job more than his beginning."* He now possessed:

- 14,000 sheep (previously 7,000)

- 6,000 camels (previously 3,000)

- 1,000 yoke of oxen (previously 500)

- 1,000 donkeys (previously 500)

He also had ten more children, seven sons and three daughters. Remarkably, his daughters received an inheritance alongside their brothers, an unusual act of economic equality in a patriarchal era.

What Made Job a Billionaire Again?

1. Faith during affliction, He didn't curse God or abandon his integrity

2. A worship lifestyle, His first response to loss was worship, which made restoration possible

3. Intercession for others, His breakthrough came when he prayed for those who judged him

4. God's covenantal justice, God rewarded Job not just for being right, but for being righteous

5. Double recompense, every area of loss was restored twofold. His story became a testimony.

Wealth Principles from Job's Life

1. Wealth must be rooted in worship. Job was a billionaire not just in business, but in faith

2. True wealth can survive loss. If everything can be taken from you, you didn't own wealth, wealth owned you

3. Character is more valuable than capital. Job's integrity was priceless

4. Never let suffering define your theology. Job refused to accuse God or believe lies

5. Restoration follows intercession. Pray for those who hurt you, your destiny may depend on it

6. Double is the reward of endurance. If you hold on in loss, God can give back more than you imagined

7. Generational inheritance matters. Job ensured his daughters were included in the legacy, an act of inclusive prosperity

8. The opinions of men must not overrule the voice of God. His friends had logic, but Job had loyalty

9. Pain refines purpose. Job came out wiser, wealthier, and more deeply connected to God

10. Tested faith is unstoppable faith. God trusted Job to go through loss and come out stronger.

Additional Lessons from Job's Story

Job's testimony is not just inspirational, it is instructional. It offers practical principles for modern billionaires and entrepreneurs of faith:

1. Build wealth on integrity, not shortcuts

2. Anchor your prosperity in worship and the fear of God

3. Diversify your resources, Job's portfolio was broad

4. Care for the poor, his righteousness protected his riches

5. Prepare for spiritual warfare, wealth draws attention

6. Respond to trials with faith, not fear

7. Trust God as your Source, not your success

8. Remain generous in loss, Job still gave emotionally and spiritually

9. Forgive those who fail you, restoration often follows mercy

10. Expect restoration, God multiplies what the enemy steals.

Job's Modern Wealth Equivalent

With 14,000 sheep, 6,000 camels, 1,000 yokes of oxen, and 1,000 donkeys, plus land, servants, and renewed influence, Job's wealth easily exceeded his former net worth. Adjusted to today's standards, his fortune could be estimated at over $20 billion, especially considering the economic impact of his livestock empire, labor force, and diversified assets.

But the actual value of Job's life was not measured in livestock, it was measured in legacy, testimony, and faith.

Conclusion: The Wealth of Resilience

Job teaches us that wealth is not just about what you have, but who you become when you lose it. He lost everything and worshiped. He was misunderstood yet remained faithful. He sat in ashes and declared hope. And when the dust settled, he emerged twice as blessed.

You may not face what Job endured, but if you have suffered loss, felt misunderstood, or battled private pain, his story is for you.

Because in God's economy, billionaires can be rebuilt, fortunes can be restored, and faith is the currency that never crashes.

CHAPTER 8

Boaz, The Righteous Capitalist

Estimated Wealth: $1 Billion

In the fields of Bethlehem, among stalks of barley and sheaves of wheat, we meet a man whose story redefines what it means to be both wealthy and righteous. His name is Boaz, a landowner, a businessman, and a benevolent patriarch. His story in the Book of Ruth presents a rare but powerful archetype: the righteous capitalist, one who understands how to accumulate wealth without abandoning morality, compassion, or covenant.

Boaz stands as a timeless model for Christian entrepreneurs and kingdom-minded investors. While others gained through exploitation or opportunism, Boaz demonstrated that profit and piety are not mutually exclusive. He operated within an economic system without being corrupted by it. He had employees, investments, and property, but he also had honor, humility, and a heart for the marginalized.

This chapter explores how Boaz became wealthy, how he stewarded that wealth with divine integrity, and what principles modern capitalists can learn from this powerful and poetic story.

A Man of Means and Morals

Boaz first appears in *Ruth 2:1* as *"a wealthy and influential man in Bethlehem."* The Hebrew phrase used here is *gibber Chayil*, which means a man of valor, substance, and integrity. His reputation preceded him, not only as a landowner but as a man of strength, character, and standing.

His wealth likely came from agricultural expansion and inheritance. He owned multiple fields, employed a workforce of reapers, and was known by name throughout the city. But more than his bank account, it was his behavior that made him righteous.

Unlike Laban, who exploited Jacob, or the rich man in Jesus' parable who ignored Lazarus, Boaz saw people, not just profit. He noticed Ruth, a foreigner gleaning in his fields, and extended compassion beyond obligation.

Boaz's brand of capitalism was not predatory, it was covenantal.

Capitalism in a Theocratic Economy

During the time of the Judges, Israel had no king, and *"everyone did what was right in their own eyes"* (Judges 21:25). Yet Boaz upheld the law of gleaning (*Leviticus 19:9–10*), which required landowners to leave the edges of their fields for the poor, widows, and foreigners.

He could have ignored this command. He could have prioritized profit. But Boaz chose to obey God's word, and even went beyond it.

When Ruth came to glean, Boaz instructed his workers to leave extra for her (*Ruth 2:15–16*). He ensured her safety, her dignity, and her provision. This is what set Boaz apart: he built a business that protected people and honored God.

In an age where the strong devoured the weak, Boaz created a pocket of economic justice.

The Business Practices of Boaz

Boaz's success wasn't accidental. He operated his business by principles we would now call faith-driven entrepreneurship.

1. **Employee Care and Spiritual Leadership**

2. When Boaz arrived in the field, his first words to his workers were, *"The Lord be with you!"* and they responded, *"The Lord bless you!"* (*Ruth 2:4*). This wasn't just a greeting; it was a culture.

3. He created an environment of respect, worship, and loyalty. In an economy dominated by survival, Boaz led with grace.

4. **Provision with Precision**

5. He didn't just let Ruth glean; he gave her access to water, instructed the men not to harass her, and ensured she left with an abundance. He didn't just give access, he gave advantage.

6. **Corporate Governance with Compassion**

7. When it came time to redeem Ruth and Naomi's family line, Boaz handled the legal process with transparency. He met with elders, followed due process, and ensured the transaction was righteous (*Ruth 4*).

8. **Asset Protection and Expansion**

9. By marrying Ruth and redeeming Elimelech's property, Boaz not only helped a family in crisis, he expanded his estate through righteous acquisition. He seized opportunities not by force, but by integrity.

Redemption Through Economics

The story of Ruth is often seen as a love story, but it is also a wealth transfer story. Naomi, who left Bethlehem full and returned bitter and empty, was restored through Boaz's generosity and obedience.

Boaz's marriage to Ruth wasn't just romantic, it was redemptive. He brought her from gleaner to owner, from outsider to matriarch. Their union gave birth to Obed, the grandfather of King David.

That means Boaz wasn't just a businessman, he became part of the Messianic lineage. His wealth wasn't just earthly, it was eternal.

Lessons from the Righteous Capitalist

Boaz's life offers enduring principles for believers seeking to navigate wealth with integrity:

1. Make room for the marginalized. Leave margins in your business for those in need. Create jobs. Offer scholarships. Sponsor single mothers. Your field should feed more than just your family.

2. Honor God's economic laws. Tithing, gleaning, and giving are not optional, they're foundational. Align your business with divine ordinances.

3. Lead with a godly culture. Bless your employees. Pray over your workplace. Build atmospheres where righteousness reigns and God is glorified.

4. Pursue profits with principles. Don't sacrifice values for value. Boaz expanded, but never exploited. You can be wealthy and godly, it's not either/or.

5. Invest in legacy, not just leverage. Boaz redeemed Ruth not just for himself, but for generations to come. Today, millions read his story, not for his fields, but for his faithfulness.

6. Be the answer to someone's famine. Ruth and Naomi were starving. Boaz's kindness fed them physically and emotionally. Kingdom capitalists see famine as a call, not a chance for gain.

Boaz in the Line of Christ

The greatest reward for Boaz's righteous capitalism was divine inclusion. *Ruth 4:21–22* lists Boaz as the father of Obed, the grandfather of Jesse, and the great-grandfather of King David.

Boaz's decision to bless a Moabite widow brought him into the royal lineage of Jesus Christ. His wealth was not wasted, it was woven into the redemptive plan of God.

Final Thoughts: Kingdom Capitalism Is Possible

Boaz is proof that you can own land, lead people, increase wealth, and still walk in holiness. You can be a capitalist and a Christian. You can hire and still honor. You can acquire and still adore the Lord.

In a world where wealth often comes at the cost of morality, Boaz reminds us that righteous capitalism is real. His story is not just about money, it's about mercy. It's about marrying the marketplace with the mandate of heaven.

Let modern billionaires learn from Boaz: your legacy is not in how much you own, but in how much you redeem. Business can be holy ground when walked with clean hands and a willing heart.

"She proves that wisdom in business is not confined by gender or geography, her enterprise sails beyond borders, and her legacy anchors in faith."

CHAPTER 9

The Proverbs 31 Millionaire

Estimated Wealth: $10–50 million

A Woman of Enterprise and International Trade

The Proverbs 31 Woman is described as one who "is like the merchant ships; she brings her food from afar" (Proverbs 31:14). This description signals far more than simple grocery shopping. It paints the portrait of a global trader, a woman engaged in import and export, supply chains, seasonal markets, and international commodities. Merchant ships in the ancient world carried spices, fabrics, oils, and metals across borders. To compare her to them is to highlight her role as a high-level entrepreneur.

She is not intimidated by scale or distance. She stretches beyond local markets to source quality goods, ensuring both profit and excellence for her household and clients. In today's world, she would be the equivalent of a businesswoman running a company with international vendors, navigating exchange rates, negotiating trade deals, and importing luxury goods for resale. Her entrepreneurial activity is not a pastime but a powerful enterprise.

This shows us that biblical womanhood does not equal financial dependence. A woman of God is not confined to consumption; she is called to production, distribution, and expansion.

Real Estate and Asset Expansion

"She considers a field and buys it; out of her earnings she plants a vineyard" (Proverbs 31:16). This single verse dismantles the myth that ancient women were excluded from real estate and capital investment. The Proverbs 31 Woman is not just managing a household budget. She is purchasing land and launching agribusiness projects.

Notice the progression. She considers a field, which implies research, valuation, negotiation, and discernment. Like a modern investor, she performs due diligence before committing capital. After purchasing the land, she plants a vineyard, turning her investment into a productive, long-term source of wealth. A vineyard means wine production, employees, distribution networks, and generational profit.

This woman does not merely earn; she multiplies her income. She transforms profits into productive assets. She refuses to consume wealth carelessly but instead establishes systems that continue generating value long after her initial effort. Her life models a timeless wealth-building principle: use current earnings to create future streams of income.

Manufacturing and Marketplace Presence

"She makes linen garments and sells them, and supplies the merchants with sashes" (Proverbs 31:24). This verse reveals her role in manufacturing and wholesale supply. She is not crafting items in obscurity but running a business that meets merchant-level demand.

This scale of work requires raw material sourcing, labor management, quality assurance, and logistics. She oversees a textile operation that employs weavers, seamstresses, and traders. The garments she produces are not for subsistence; they are refined goods that command value in the marketplace.

She is unafraid to step into the public square with her products. Her brand is visible, profitable, and scalable. This teaches us that excellence must be paired with positioning. Even the best product holds no power without access to the right market.

Leadership at Home and in the Community

"She watches over the affairs of her household and does not eat the bread of idleness" (Proverbs 31:27). Despite her business achievements, she does not neglect her home. She governs her household with excellence, proving herself both an entrepreneur and a household executive.

Her home is clothed in scarlet, her family is protected against the cold, and her children rise to call her blessed (verses 21 and 28). Her husband praises her in public, showing that her private diligence produces public honor. She embodies what many modern leaders struggle to attain: balance without burnout.

This balance is possible because she operates through planning and delegation. She builds systems that sustain both her home and her enterprise. Her leadership is not reactive but intentional. In contemporary terms, she runs a corporation while raising the next generation of leaders in her family.

Her Brand, Her Worth

"She is clothed with strength and dignity; she can laugh at the days to come" (Proverbs 31:25). Her brand rests on values, not vanity. She is known for strength, dignity, and wisdom. Her laughter at the future demonstrates peace of mind born from preparation and foresight.

She is not anxious about inflation, recessions, or shortages, because she has prepared in advance. Her life echoes the wisdom of the ant, gathering during harvest to endure through winter.

Her internal strength flows from her fear of the Lord, and her external strength is reflected in confidence and presentation. Her name carries weight, her products carry excellence, and her presence carries respect.

15 Wealth-Building Lessons from the Proverbs 31 Woman

1. Vision precedes venture. She plans before acting.

2. Diligence multiplies income. Her hands are never idle.

3. Invest in assets, not liabilities. She buys land instead of luxuries.

4. Global thinking expands reach. She trades with distant markets.

5. Diversify income streams. She engages in agriculture, textiles, and commerce.

6. Integrate faith into finance. Her fear of the Lord directs her choices.

7. Build systems, not stress. She creates efficiency through planning.

8. Train the next generation. Her children inherit her mindset.

9. Earn before spending. She plants from her earnings.

10. Brand with values. Strength and dignity define her.

11. Prepare for economic shifts. She is ready for winter.

12. Be visible in business. She engages merchants and public platforms.

13. Excel in quality. Her goods are desirable.

14. Build with purpose. Her wealth flows from wisdom.

15. Balance is possible. She thrives in both business and family life.

A Final Look at Her Worth

"Charm is deceptive, and beauty is fleeting, but a woman who fears the Lord is to be praised" (Proverbs 31:30). Her net worth lies not only in financial assets but in her character. Yet her character fuels her competence. She is holy, strategic, and visionary. Her fear of the Lord grants her wisdom, which she applies to business and leadership alike.

In today's terms, she would be a self-made millionaire with diversified investments, international trade partnerships, real estate holdings, manufacturing operations, community influence, and a respected brand. Yet she would operate with humility and grace.

The Proverbs 31 Woman proves that biblical womanhood is not weak, dependent, or passive. It is powerful, resourceful, wealthy, and spiritual. She is not a distant ideal but a prophetic model of what happens when godliness and strategy meet.

"True wealth is not only measured in treasures amassed, but in a generation restored to righteousness."

CHAPTER 10

King Josiah, The Billionaire Reformer

Estimated Wealth: $6 Billion

A Throne at Eight, a Vision Beyond His Years

Josiah began his reign at the age of eight, following the assassination of his father, Amon, a king who had led Judah into idolatry and corruption. What Josiah inherited was not just a throne but a nation in spiritual and social collapse.

By the time he was sixteen, Josiah had set his heart on seeking the God of David. By the age of twenty, he was tearing down altars to Baal, cutting down Asherah poles, and cleansing Jerusalem of idolatry. His pursuit of righteousness was matched by remarkable administrative strength, which laid the foundation for both national stability and economic consolidation.

Josiah's vision went far beyond survival. He wanted renewal. His reign was not defined by conquest or expansion, but by restoration and reform.

Restoring the Temple and Reclaiming the Treasure

One of Josiah's most transformative acts was the restoration of the Temple in Jerusalem (2 Kings 22). Once the pride of Israel, the Temple had been neglected, polluted, and stripped of its holiness. Josiah commanded that the silver collected at the Temple gates be used to rebuild the house of God.

This project was no cosmetic upgrade. It employed skilled builders, carpenters, and artisans. It restored dignity to the nation's spiritual center. Most importantly, it led to the rediscovery of the Book of the Law, which sparked a nationwide revival.

Here lies one of Josiah's most significant insights: spiritual order fuels economic order. By restoring the altar, he restored the economy. By rebuilding the Temple, he rebuilt trust in God.

Josiah's Economic Strength and Fiscal Policies

The Bible does not give us a ledger of Josiah's financial strategies, but history and Scripture suggest several key practices that produced immense wealth and stability:

Temple Taxation and Offerings

With the Temple restored, it flourished. Tithes, offerings, and temple taxes created a steady flow of resources into Judah's treasury, reinforcing both national and spiritual strength.

Direct Investment into Labor

Josiah placed funds directly in the hands of workers, masons, carpenters, and artisans, without oppressive oversight. Scripture records, "they dealt faithfully" (2 Kings 22:7). This created an economy rooted in integrity and trust.

Peace Producing Prosperity

Unlike David, Josiah did not reign in wartime. His years of peace freed resources for infrastructure, worship, and development. Just as Solomon's peaceful era allowed wealth to multiply, Josiah's reign proved that prosperity thrives in stability.

Through these systems, Josiah oversaw a treasury valued at the equivalent of $6 billion. Yet his true riches were in national revival, spiritual integrity, and divine favor.

Wealth Lessons from Josiah's Life

Josiah's story offers a blueprint for modern wealth-builders who long to steward resources with righteousness:

1. **Spiritual Renewal Precedes Economic Revival**

2. Josiah started with God, not with gold. When the land was cleansed of idols, blessings followed.

3. **Direct Investment Builds Legacy**

4. Josiah spent resources on temples, workers, and community renewal. Lasting wealth comes from building what outlives you.

5. **Trust Multiplies Wealth**

    By empowering faithful workers without micromanagement, Josiah created a culture of honor that encouraged prosperity.

6. **Leadership Is Stewardship**

7. True wealth is not possession but responsibility. Josiah saw himself as a steward of Judah's resources, not their owner.

8. **Obedience Is Greater than Strategy**

9. After reading the rediscovered Book of the Law, Josiah tore his garments in grief. He did not hide behind his wealth or position. He humbled himself, repented, and led the nation back to the covenant. His reforms remind us that obedience is the highest form of leadership.

A Billionaire's Final Battle

Josiah's end was tragic. He died in battle against Pharaoh Necho, despite warnings not to engage. Whether this was a miscalculation or an act of faith remains debated. Yet his legacy was not defined by his final battle but by his reforms.

Scripture testifies that "neither before nor after Josiah was there a king like him who turned to the Lord with all his heart and with all his soul and with all his strength" (2 Kings 23:25). His life was proof that even in youth, bold obedience can shake nations.

A Modern Call to Reformation Wealth

Today's world needs Josiahs, leaders in business, government, ministry, and finance who will rise to confront idolatry, corruption, and broken systems. Wealth is not for comfort alone. It is for reformation. It is for rebuilding the places where truth has been silenced and righteousness has been forgotten.

You do not need to be old to carry wisdom or experienced to make an impact. You need a surrendered heart, a courageous spirit, and a mission that aligns with God's purposes.

Final Thoughts: Rebuild. Reform. Reap.

King Josiah's life proves that wealth is a servant to worship and leadership is stewardship. He did not build the largest palace or compose the most psalms, but he revived a nation, redirected billions toward God's house, and left a legacy of righteousness.

You can do the same. Your calling is not to chase money but to chase mission. When mission aligns with heaven, wealth will follow.

CHAPTER 11

The Wise Men, Wealthy Worshippers from the East

Estimated Worth: $2 Billion

The story of Jesus' birth is one of the most celebrated and widely told events in human history. Yet within this miraculous narrative lies the appearance of mysterious figures often referred to as the Wise Men or Magi, whose actions hold profound lessons on wealth, worship, and divine assignment. Their visit was not simply ceremonial; it was an economically significant, spiritually strategic act that announced the intersection of treasure and truth.

Though their presence in Scripture is brief, the implications of their journey are far-reaching. They brought gold, frankincense, and myrrh, three rare, high-value commodities that represent more than just gifts. They represent an offering of wealth at the feet of divinity. These were not ordinary travelers; they were highly educated, politically influential, and materially affluent men who recognized spiritual truth and responded with extravagant generosity.

Who Were the Wise Men?

The Gospel of Matthew is the only biblical account that records their journey (*Matthew 2:1 12*), but historical sources give insight into their identity. The term *Magi* refers to a priestly caste of ancient Persian or Babylonian astrologers, scholars, and dream interpreters. They were known for their knowledge of astronomy, mathematics, medicine, and prophecy.

Their influence in royal courts made them kingmakers, advisors to emperors and rulers in the East. Traveling in caravans, these men would not have arrived alone.

They came with soldiers, attendants, and a large procession worthy of their rank. Their appearance in Jerusalem caused a stir, signaling that these were not obscure mystics but powerful, visible dignitaries whose presence demanded attention.

They were wealthy men not only because of their personal possessions but also because of their influence, resources, and authority. Their long and costly journey to see a newborn King exemplifies the principle that true wealth is not just in possessing riches but in being willing to release it for divine purposes.

Their journey: Purposeful and Prophetic

The journey of the Wise Men was not impulsive; it was planned, strategic, and prophetic. They followed a celestial sign, commonly referred to as the *Star of Bethlehem*. This star guided them to the place where Jesus was born.

The act of following a star is symbolic of people who pursue divine revelation despite inconvenience, uncertainty, or cultural opposition. Their journey would have taken weeks or months. It involved crossing borders, facing bandits, engaging in political negotiations, and overcoming spiritual resistance. Yet they pressed forward. Why? Because wealthy worshippers are willing to invest time, energy, and money to encounter God.

This challenges the modern mindset that seeks convenience in worship. The Wise Men demonstrate that sacrifice is a companion to significance. They did not wait for Jesus to come to them; they pursued Him until they found Him.

Their Gifts: Economic and Symbolic Value

The gold, frankincense, and myrrh presented to Jesus were not random. Each gift was laden with both monetary and prophetic value.

1. **Gold** – A universal symbol of wealth, royalty, and stability. Gold represented Jesus' kingship and also served as a financial provision for Joseph and Mary's upcoming escape to Egypt. Some scholars believe that the family's ability to flee and survive in a foreign land was due to the monetary value of these gifts.

2. **Frankincense** – A rare resin used in priestly worship and temple rituals. It symbolized Jesus' divine nature and priestly role. Economically, frankincense was expensive and often used by the wealthy for fragrance, healing, and worship.

3. **Myrrh** – A valuable embalming agent used for burial. It foreshadowed Jesus' death and suffering. Like frankincense, myrrh was rare and costly, often worth more than its weight in gold.

Each gift represented a facet of Christ's identity: King (*Gold*), Priest (*Frankincense*), and Sacrifice (*Myrrh*). But beyond their symbolism, the gifts were acts of resource allocation. The Wise Men gave what was precious to them to the One they deemed worthy.

Wealth at the Feet of Worship

The Wise Men embody a vital principle of kingdom economics: wealth finds its highest expression when laid at the feet of divine purpose. These men could have used their treasures for personal gain, political leverage, or religious ritual. Instead, they gave it to a baby who had no palace, no army, no throne, but carried the destiny of redemption.

They teach us that worship is incomplete without offering. In many cultures, the act of giving precedes dialogue with royalty or a deity. The Wise Men gave not as a bribe but as a recognition. They acknowledged Jesus' worth by offering their best.

This is the heart of true worship: recognizing divine value and responding with extravagant giving. They also reveal the truth that material wealth should flow in the direction of prophetic destiny. Their giving ensured that the child King would survive the political threats of Herod and fulfill His calling.

Lessons in Strategic Giving

The Wise Men offer more than a Christmas story; they provide a template of strategic giving:

1. Discern the timing of your gift – They gave when the child was most vulnerable, yet destined for greatness.

2. Give to what aligns with heaven's plan – They followed God's guidance, not public opinion.[3]

3. Give sacrificially, not casually – Their journey and gifts cost them much.

4. Their generosity followed divine illumination.

5. Give without expecting return – They gave and left quietly, without fanfare.

6. Fund the future – Their gifts enabled Jesus' escape from Herod and sustained His family in exile.

In a world obsessed with returns, the Magi gave without demand. They remind us that kingdom giving is an investment in eternity, not in ego.

From Wisdom to Worship: The Wealth Mindset

The Wise Men were not merely rich; they were wise. They understood that wealth without worship is hollow. Their journey teaches us that the truly wealthy are those who recognize when to bow, where to give, and how to honor divine purpose.

---

[3] The Wise Men's gifts (Matthew 2:11) symbolized more than wealth, they reflected worship, honor, and foresight. True prosperity blends resources with reverence.

In today's terms, the Wise Men would be global thought leaders, investors, and philanthropists. They would be CEOs, university deans, and Nobel laureates who understand that intellect is not divorced from worship. Their story affirms that wealth and wisdom are not mutually exclusive but mutually empowering when governed by truth.

The Economics of Kingdom Worship

Their example also gives insight into the economics of kingdom worship:

- Direction precedes donation – A star guided them. Revelation governs release.

- Proximity enhances purpose – They brought their treasure near to the child, not just to a cause.

- Protection follows provision – God warned them in a dream not to return to Herod. Their obedience preserved them.

- Provision empowers purpose – Their gifts financed God's plan for Jesus' early survival.

They show us that when we align our wealth with worship, we step into divine protection, direction, and promotion.

Prophetic Implications

The visit of the Wise Men was not just an act of generosity; it was a prophetic act that signaled the inclusion of the Gentile nations into the redemptive story of Christ.

It was a foreshadowing of Isaiah 60:3, which says, *"Nations will come to your light, and kings to the brightness of your dawn."* They came from the East, representing the nations.

They bowed to a Jewish Messiah, representing reconciliation. They brought wealth, representing the transfer of resources for kingdom expansion.

In their journey, we see the beginning of the wealth of nations flowing into God's redemptive plan.

It is a pattern that continues today: entrepreneurs, investors, and nations aligning their resources with righteous purpose.

Final Reflections: Kingdom Investors

The Wise Men are more than nativity characters. They are kingdom investors who understood the power of prophetic giving. Their wealth did not define them; what they did with it did.

They remind us that the highest form of wealth is not accumulation but allocation. They journeyed, worshipped, gave, and disappeared, but their story still shapes how we think about giving, worship, and divine alignment.

Their legacy teaches that:

- You are never too rich to bow before God.

- No journey is too long when the goal is a divine purpose.

- No gift is too great when it honors the King.

"Some fortunes are not measured in what they display, but in the courage to invest in eternity at the darkest hour."

CHAPTER 12

Joseph of Arimathea, The Hidden Billionaire Who Honored the King

Estimated Worth: $35 Million

Among the many personalities who shaped the biblical narrative of Jesus' life, few are as intriguing and paradoxical as Joseph of Arimathea. A man of enormous influence and affluence, he appears in all four Gospels but remains wrapped in mystery.

Joseph was not a loud disciple, nor was he one of the Twelve. Yet at the darkest moment in history, when even Jesus' closest followers had fled, Joseph stepped forward with boldness and wealth to honor the crucified Christ. This act of courage and generosity reveals much about the kind of man Joseph was. He was a *rich man,* as *Matthew 27:57* clearly states, but he was more than rich; he was righteous.

He was a man of authority, yet humble. He moved in elite circles, yet was not consumed by them. He was a member of the Sanhedrin, the Jewish ruling council, but he opposed their condemnation of Jesus. Above all, he used his wealth not for show but for significance. His story illustrates how silent wealth can become a loud testimony when used at the right moment. Through his life, we discover kingdom principles about stewardship, courage, honor, and divine timing.

A Man of Wealth and Integrity

Joseph is first described as *"a rich man from Arimathea, who had himself become a disciple of Jesus"* (*Matthew 27:57*). The word *rich* used here comes from the Greek term *plosions,* implying vast material resources. He was not simply wealthy; he was extraordinarily wealthy.

Early church traditions suggest he was a landowner and possibly involved in the lucrative tin trade between the Middle East and the British Isles, which would have made him internationally wealthy.

But Joseph's wealth was not his only notable trait. *Mark 15:43* describes him as *"a respected member of the council, who was also himself looking for the kingdom of God."* He was part of the very body that condemned Jesus, yet *Luke 23:50–51* tells us that he *"had not consented to their decision and action."*

This marks Joseph as a man of integrity. He stood against the majority even when it could have cost him his reputation, position, or life. He did not chase popularity; he pursued righteousness. He was waiting for the kingdom of God, not the praises of men. Integrity must precede influence. Without it, wealth becomes toxic. With character, wealth becomes a tool for divine impact.

Boldness at the Cross

When Jesus died on the cross, His body hung lifeless and exposed. According to Roman custom, crucified criminals were often left to rot or thrown into mass graves. The shame of crucifixion extended even beyond death.

Yet Joseph of Arimathea would not allow such indignity to stain the Savior's legacy. In an extraordinary act of boldness, Joseph approached Pilate and asked for Jesus' body (*Mark 15:43*). This was no small request. Associating oneself with an executed *insurrectionist* could provoke suspicion, political backlash, and religious ostracism.

Yet Joseph did not hesitate. It takes courage to use wealth for a cause that may cost you everything. Joseph used his political access and social capital to honor Jesus, knowing full well that it could ruin him in the eyes of Rome or the Sanhedrin. Pilate, surprised that Jesus was already dead, verified the matter with the centurion and granted Joseph permission. This gave Joseph the privilege of handling the body of the Messiah.

His wealth was not a shield for comfort but a sword for purpose.

The Tomb of Honor

John 19:41 tells us, *"At the place where Jesus was crucified, there was a garden, and in the garden a new tomb, in which no one had ever been laid."* This tomb belonged to Joseph.

It was a newly hewn cave, carved from rock at great expense, in an affluent area near Golgotha. This was not an ordinary grave but a tomb fit for nobility. Carved rock tombs were prestigious, expensive, and typically reserved for generations of wealthy families.

That Joseph gave his tomb to Jesus was no small matter. He gave the best he had, not leftovers. He honored Christ not with convenience but with costly generosity.

Isaiah 53:9 had prophetically declared, *"He was assigned a grave with the wicked, and with the rich in his death."* Joseph unknowingly fulfilled this prophecy. In giving his tomb, he ensured that Jesus would not be buried among criminals but with the wealthy and honored.

Kingdom wealth is positioning resources at the intersection of prophecy and purpose.

Wealth Stored for Purpose

Joseph's actions teach us that wealth must be stored for purpose, not just security. Had he squandered his riches on vanity or excess, he would not have been positioned to provide for the Messiah's burial. But his resources were available and ready.

He had access to political power, land, and materials, and when the moment came, he did not hesitate. This challenges us to think of stewardship as strategic readiness. Joseph was not flashy, but he was faithful. He was not loud, but he was leveraged. Sometimes God calls us to prepare resources for purposes we do not yet understand.

A Silent but Strategic Disciple

Unlike the apostles, Joseph was not in the spotlight. He was a quiet disciple, perhaps even secretive due to his position (*John 19:38* says he followed Jesus secretly for fear of the Jews). Yet when the time came to act, he stepped out of the shadows into significance.

Kingdom billionaires do not always lead revivals or preach sermons. Some fund movements. Some provide burial space. Some open doors. God uses quiet financiers as powerfully as vocal preachers.

Joseph reminds us that your assignment does not require applause, it requires obedience.

Partnership with Nicodemus

Joseph was not alone in this mission. John's Gospel records that Nicodemus, another member of the Sanhedrin, accompanied him. Nicodemus brought 75 pounds of myrrh and aloes, an incredibly lavish gift.

Together, these two influential men, both wealthy and from elite circles, performed the burial rites for Jesus. Their partnership demonstrates the power of collaborative wealth in the kingdom. Joseph provided the tomb; Nicodemus brought the spices. Neither gift was more important than the other.

God often pairs people of means for greater impact. The kingdom flourishes when stewards unite under one vision.

Kingdom Lessons from Joseph of Arimathea

Joseph of Arimathea provides a rich treasury of lessons for modern wealth builders:

1. Wealth is a tool, not an identity.

2. Be ready for kingdom assignments.

3. Boldness activates provision.

4. Use your influence to shift outcomes.

5. Be willing to sacrifice for truth.

6. Do not wait for public applause.

7. Fund holy transitions.

8. Prepare for divine disruptions.

9. Partner with others for impact.

10. Store wealth with purpose.

11. Legacy is shaped by obedience.

12. Fulfill prophecy by faithfulness.

13. Let righteousness guide your riches.

14. Honor the King, even in silence.

15. Understand timing.

Legacy of a Hidden Billionaire

Joseph disappears from the biblical record after Jesus' burial, yet his legacy continues. He is remembered not for his business empire but for one defining act: honoring Jesus in death.

This is the paradox of kingdom wealth, it is remembered not for accumulation but for allocation.

Some traditions claim that Joseph later became a missionary to Britain, bringing the gospel westward. Others say he founded churches and spread the resurrection message. While these accounts are debated, his biblical role is clear: he used his wealth to steward Christ's body, preparing the way for resurrection.

What an honor. What a legacy. He did not write a Gospel, but his actions helped fulfill one. He did not preach the resurrection, but he facilitated the space where it happened.

Joseph of Arimathea reminds us that kingdom greatness is not always about visibility, it is about responsibility. He was a silent disciple who showed up when it counted most. He used his money to honor the King. He leveraged his access to influence outcomes. He gave sacrificially, strategically, and significantly.

In today's world, where wealth is often idolized or demonized, Joseph provides a balanced picture. He was wealthy, yes, but also holy, wise, and courageous. He proves that you can be both rich and righteous, both powerful and principled.

His story compels us to ask: *What am I storing my wealth for? Am I preparing my resources for eternal impact? Will I be ready when divine purpose knocks?*

Joseph of Arimathea was ready. And because he was, the Son of God received a burial of honor, only to rise in glory.

"The truest riches of a nation are unlocked when its leader restores both its treasure and its truth to God."

CHAPTER 13

King Josiah, The Billionaire Reformer

Estimated Wealth: $6 Billion

Among the kings of Judah, one name stands out not only for his youthful ascension to the throne but also for his righteous zeal and bold reforms: **King Josiah**. Unlike Solomon, whose wealth was legendary, or David, who expanded the kingdom through war and worship, Josiah's riches lay in the power of reform, restoration, and revival. Yet his physical wealth was equally impressive, estimated by scholars to rival over *$6 billion* in today's terms through centralized governance, taxation, temple treasuries, and recovered offerings.

Josiah's story isn't just about fiscal abundance. It's about what happens when a leader places both treasure and truth under the authority of God. His rule teaches us that wealth isn't only built through economic transactions, it can also be multiplied by spiritual alignment, national vision, and courageous leadership.

1. A Throne at Eight, a Vision Beyond His Years

Josiah began his reign at the age of eight after the assassination of his father, Amon, a wicked king. Despite his young age, Josiah would become one of the greatest reformers in Judah's history. He didn't inherit just a throne; he inherited a kingdom riddled with idolatry, corruption, and spiritual decay.

By age sixteen, Josiah began to seek after the God of David. By age twenty, he began purging Judah and Jerusalem of altars to Baal, Asherah poles, and all forms of idol worship. His pursuit of righteousness was matched with astounding administrative courage, which laid the foundation for national stability and financial consolidation.

2. Restoring the Temple, Reclaiming the Treasure

One of Josiah's boldest moves was the restoration of the Temple in Jerusalem (*2 Kings 22*). The Temple had been neglected, defiled, and stripped of its spiritual significance under prior kings. Josiah ordered that the funds collected at the temple doors, silver offerings from the people, be used not for royal splendor but for rebuilding the house of God.

This was not a minor renovation. The project employed skilled laborers, stonecutters, carpenters, and artisans. Josiah redirected national funds toward spiritual revival, a move that did not deplete Judah's wealth but revived its moral economy. In fact, rediscovering God's law during the temple repairs ignited the greatest national repentance in centuries.

We learn here that reform and restoration are economically catalytic. When spiritual order is reestablished, financial systems stabilize. Josiah understood that a prosperous kingdom required more than trade routes, it needed a righteous altar.

3. Josiah's Economic Strength and Fiscal Policies

While the Bible doesn't give explicit line-by-line figures of Josiah's economic strategy, contextual analysis suggests several means by which his kingdom generated and managed immense wealth:

a) Temple Taxation and Offerings

Josiah reinstituted the collection of tithes, temple taxes, and offerings, money that flowed directly into the national treasury, once the temple was restored, thereby increasing the national treasury. Religious restoration fueled economic circulation.

b) Redistribution of Resources

Josiah ordered that money be placed directly into the hands of the workers, masons, builders, carpenters, without micromanagement. The

Scripture notes, *"they dealt faithfully"* (*2 Kings 22:7*), proving that honor systems can fuel trust economies.

c) Military Peace Leading to Surplus

Josiah did not rule during active war campaigns like his ancestors. His peaceful reign allowed funds to be directed toward infrastructure, social development, and spiritual institutions, much like Solomon's non-war years.

It's estimated that through these systems, Josiah governed a treasury worth the equivalent of *$6 billion*, and even more in national goodwill, religious unity, and prophetic momentum.

4. Wealth Lessons from Josiah's Life

Josiah offers a blueprint not only for restoring nations but also for governing wealth with integrity. Lessons every modern wealth-builder should consider:

1. Spiritual renewal precedes economic revival.
2. Direct investment in infrastructure matters.
3. Wealth must be managed with trust.
4. Leadership is a stewardship of resources.

5. Spiritual Boldness Over Political Caution

What truly separates Josiah from others is his radical obedience to God, even when it disrupted political traditions. After reading the Book of the Law (discovered during temple repairs), Josiah tore his garments in grief.

He didn't make excuses for national disobedience. He didn't hide behind his wealth. He humbled himself. Then, he gathered the people and publicly renewed the covenant. He reinstated the Passover, cleansed the land, and silenced every form of idolatry.

His actions reversed decades of decline in just a few short years. This reveals a profound truth: God can rebuild what took generations to destroy when a leader fully yields.

6. A Billionaire's Final Battle

Josiah's death was tragic but instructive. He died in battle against Pharaoh Necho, even after being warned. Some scholars debate whether Josiah's boldness in that battle was a misstep or an act of faith.

Either way, his legacy was sealed, not by his final mistake but by the reforms he sparked. He was remembered as a king who turned to

God with all his heart, soul, and might (*2 Kings 23:25*). No king before or after matched his zeal for reform.

7. A Modern Call to Reformation Wealth

Today, we need Josiahs in business, in government, in ministry, and in finance, people who will see the broken systems, the corrupted temples, and the idols of materialism, and rise to restore.

Your wealth is not just about comfort. It's about reformation. It's about rebuilding the places where truth has fallen and righteousness has been neglected. Josiah teaches us that you don't have to be old to be wise, or seasoned to be significant. You need a surrendered heart, a courageous spirit, and a willingness to steward God's purposes with boldness.

Final Thoughts: Rebuild. Reform. Reap.

King Josiah stands as one of history's most excellent reminders that wealth must serve worship and that leadership must prioritize legacy over luxury. He didn't build the most enormous palace. He didn't write the most psalms. But he shook a nation, revived a people, and redirected billions toward the glory of God.

You can do the same. Let Josiah's legacy stirs your own. You don't need more money; you need more mission. And when mission aligns with heaven, the money will follow.

"A true guardian of wealth is not one who hoards it, but one who preserves it through wisdom, faith, and foresight."

CHAPTER 14

Hezekiah, The Guardian of National Wealth

Estimated Wealth: $20 Billion

In the annals of biblical kings, **Hezekiah** stands apart as a ruler whose prosperity was matched by his piety, and whose leadership elevated a nation economically, spiritually, and politically. As king of Judah, he inherited a kingdom teetering on the edge of collapse, pressured by foreign powers, marred by spiritual compromise, and plagued by fiscal decay.

But within his reign, Judah witnessed one of its most significant periods of national recovery, both spiritually and financially. Hezekiah was not merely a royal figure; he was a guardian of national wealth. He exemplified the role of a godly statesman who managed the treasures of a nation with wisdom, faith, and foresight.

Through strategic reforms, military preparation, spiritual restoration, and a profound reliance on God, Hezekiah stabilized the economy and preserved national assets in the face of looming disaster. His story reveals how righteous leadership can turn a bankrupt system into a blessed storehouse, and how failing to handle prosperity with discretion can open doors to danger.

This chapter explores Hezekiah's role in managing the collective wealth of Judah, the lessons from his stewardship, and the critical balance between divine favor and financial responsibility.

A Prosperous Beginning

Hezekiah began his reign at the age of twenty-five and ruled for twenty-nine years (*2 Kings 18:2*). From the outset, he distinguished himself from his predecessors by returning the kingdom to God. *"He did what was right in the eyes of the Lord, just as his father David had done"* (*2 Kings 18:3*).

His first act as king was not economic but spiritual. He purged the land of idols, repaired the temple, and reinstituted worship. The spiritual climate of the nation directly impacted its financial health, and Hezekiah understood this.

By restoring the priesthood and temple operations, he reignited the divine economy that had long been dormant. The people responded with generosity. According to *2 Chronicles 31:5-10*, the people brought in such an abundance of first fruits, tithes, and offerings that they had to stack the wealth in heaps.

The high priest told Hezekiah, *"Since the people began to bring their contributions to the temple of the Lord, we have had enough to eat and plenty to spare."* This was not mere fundraising; it was an economic revival rooted in worship. Hezekiah tied the financial future of the nation to its reverence for God.

National Defense and Infrastructure Development

Hezekiah was not only a spiritual reformer; he was an infrastructure strategist and master planner. When the threat of Assyrian invasion loomed, he didn't panic. He acted with precision and preparation.

One of his most notable achievements was the construction of **Hezekiah's Tunnel**, a 1,750-foot conduit carved through solid rock to secure water access inside the city walls during siege. This engineering marvel, still intact today, is a testament to his foresight. By protecting the city's most vital resource, Hezekiah ensured national resilience in crisis.

He also fortified Jerusalem, built new walls, reinforced towers, and produced weapons in abundance *(2 Chronicles 32:5)*. These were not random actions. Hezekiah understood that wealth must be defended. Prosperity without protection is vulnerability.

His defensive measures were economic safeguards. A city under siege could not trade, worship, or grow. Hezekiah's vision was clear: secure the supply lines, and you secure the future.

The Storehouses of Judah

Hezekiah's financial acumen is most visible in *2 Chronicles 32:27 29*:

"Hezekiah had very great riches and honor, and he made treasuries for his silver and gold and for his precious stones, spices, shields, and all kinds of valuables. He also made storehouses for the harvest of grain, new wine and oil; and stalls for all kinds of cattle, and pens for the flocks."

This is a stunning image of nationalized wealth management. Hezekiah wasn't content with accumulating wealth, he preserved it. He built multiple layers of storage and defense:

1. Diversified storage encompasses not just money, but also grain, oil, wine, and livestock.

2. Distributed infrastructure, not one vault, but multiple centers of wealth.

3. Domestic productivity, wealth was produced internally, not imported.

Hezekiah shows us that wealth isn't just about earning, it's about preserving, diversifying, and systematizing resources. These are timeless principles for nations, organizations, and individuals alike.

Trusting in the Lord and Not the Enemy

Despite all his planning, Hezekiah never placed his trust in the structures of men. When King Sennacherib of Assyria invaded Judah and threatened Jerusalem, Hezekiah did not buckle. Instead, he sought the counsel of Isaiah the prophet and humbled himself in prayer.

Most rulers would respond with treaties or tributes. Hezekiah responded with intercession. He laid the threatening letter from the Assyrians before God in the temple and prayed (*2 Kings 19:14–19*).

This act of vulnerability brought divine intervention: the angel of the Lord struck down 185,000 Assyrian soldiers in one night.

This account reveals a powerful truth: strategic wealth is no substitute for spiritual authority. Hezekiah had prepared in the natural, but his ultimate defense came through divine power.

The Babylonian Error: When Wealth Becomes Vanity

However, Hezekiah's story also includes a cautionary tale. After his miraculous healing and national victory, envoys from Babylon came to visit him. Instead of glorifying God, Hezekiah proudly showed them all his treasures, his storehouses, armory, and wealth (*2 Kings 20:13*).

This display of vanity would cost the nation. Isaiah rebuked him, declaring that the Babylonians would one day carry everything away into exile. The wealth he flaunted would become the prize of plunder.

Here, we learn a critical lesson: never expose what should be secured. Wealth can attract favor or become a target, depending on how it is handled. Hezekiah's lapse was not in having wealth, but in using it as a trophy instead of a testimony.

Lessons in Wealth Stewardship from Hezekiah

1. Revival precedes wealth, spiritual restoration unlocked economic abundance.

2. Protect your pipelines, secure resources like water, food, and energy.

3. Build for the future, storehouses preserve wealth for times of crisis.

4. National wealth requires national worship, God is the ultimate blesser.

5. Discretion is defense, don't boast about blessings to the wrong audience.

6. Leadership must be prophetic; he sought counsel from Isaiah.

7. Prayers protect assets, divine power thwarted economic disaster.

8. Create systems, not just savings, his infrastructure outlasted his reign.

9. Wealth without wisdom invites judgment, Babylon came for what he showed.

10. Honor God with your increase, Hezekiah's early success came from alignment.

Legacy and the Weight of a Nation

Hezekiah's reign left behind more than treasuries. He left a legacy of governance rooted in God, integrity, and long-term planning. His son, Manasseh, would sadly undo much of the spiritual foundation, but the remnants of Hezekiah's reforms continued to influence Judah.

Hezekiah remains one of the few kings of Judah praised not only for his faith but for his financial and political intelligence. He didn't just collect gold, he created systems to protect national inheritance.

In a modern world of economic volatility, corrupt leadership, and moral compromise, Hezekiah stands as a beacon: you can lead with righteousness, govern with vision, and still prosper beyond measure.

Final Thoughts: A King Who Understood Kingdom Economics

Hezekiah shows us that national wealth is not just a number on paper, it's a product of policy, prayer, and prophetic wisdom. He was a guardian not merely of gold, but of legacy. He didn't waste the wealth of the nation; he multiplied and managed it.

He prepared for the siege and sowed into revival. And even in failure, he teaches us that wealth must be held with humility, not hubris.

In a generation of personal accumulation, Hezekiah reminds us of the power of collective stewardship. He didn't just make himself rich, he made the nation resilient. And that, perhaps, is the highest honor of any biblical billionaire: not how much they possessed, but how well they protected and positioned it for purpose.

CHAPTER 15

Laban, The Opportunist

Estimated Wealth: $1 Billion

In the complex fabric of biblical billionaires, Laban occupies a controversial but instructive role. Unlike Abraham or Job, whose wealth was marked by covenant and character, Laban's prosperity was built on opportunity, manipulation, and cunning negotiation. He was a wealthy patriarch, a shrewd businessman, and a master of economic leverage. His story, interwoven with the journey of Jacob, offers a cautionary tale of how the pursuit of wealth without honor can yield temporary success but long-term fallout.

Laban is not celebrated for righteousness or generosity, yet his financial acumen cannot be overlooked. He built a sizable estate, managed vast herds and flocks, had control over multiple laborers, and orchestrated marriage alliances that furthered his reach. What Laban lacked in spiritual integrity, he compensated for in strategic positioning and shrewd economics. He represents the worldly billionaire, those who use circumstances to their advantage, often at the expense of others. While his methods were questionable, Laban's rise and reign in the economy of ancient Haran contain valuable insights. This chapter examines how he grew his wealth, the lessons from his dealings with Jacob, and the spiritual consequences of profit without principle.

Wealth by Circumstance, Not Covenant

Laban, son of Bethuel and brother of Rebekah, first appears in *Genesis 24*, where he plays a key role in negotiating the marriage of his sister to Abraham's servant on behalf of Isaac. Even in this early interaction, Laban's eyes are drawn more to the gold and gifts than to the sacredness of the moment. *Genesis 24:29–30* says: *"As soon as he saw the ring, and the bracelets upon his sister's hands… he ran out unto the man."*

This foreshadowed Laban's orientation toward material gain over spiritual significance. He didn't become wealthy through divine promise but through his skill in negotiation and opportunistic behavior. By the time Jacob arrives in Haran (*Genesis 29*), Laban is already established as a man with servants, flocks, and daughters, proof of a thriving estate. His wealth wasn't given by divine decree; it was accumulated through calculated relationships, including using his daughters as leverage and his nephew Jacob as unpaid labor.

The Jacob Deal: Labor Without Wages

When Jacob fled to Laban after deceiving Esau, he offered to work seven years in exchange for Laban's daughter Rachel. Laban agreed, but when the time came, he deceptively gave Jacob Leah instead. This bait-and-switch not only exploited Jacob's passion but also locked him into fourteen years of labor.

Here, Laban reveals a core strategy: exploit emotional leverage to gain economic advantage. He capitalized on Jacob's love to secure a long-term laborer without fair compensation. Even after Jacob agreed to work an additional seven years, Laban changed his wages ten times (*Genesis 31:7*). He continuously adjusted the terms in his favor, always finding a way to preserve his prosperity at Jacob's expense.

This kind of manipulation reveals a lesson: not all wealth is just, and not all employers are fair. Laban's fortune grew because of Jacob's anointing, yet he never intended to share that blessing equitably.

Laban's Flocks Multiply

Despite his deceptive practices, Laban's livestock, herds, and influence multiplied. The increase came not from Laban's labor but from Jacob's management and the favor of God on Jacob's life. In *Genesis 30*, Jacob proposed a deal to separate the speckled and spotted animals as his wages. Laban, thinking the deal was to his advantage, agreed.

But God gave Jacob wisdom to breed stronger animals, and soon Jacob's flocks began to outpace Laban's. This reversal frustrated Laban. It exposed a flaw in his model, he could control a man, but not the hand of God. His wealth plateaued while Jacob's soared. This shift in economic power reveals that favor can override manipulation.

Key Wealth Lessons from Laban's Rise and Fall

Though Laban was not a moral example, his story offers key principles for both caution and wisdom:

1. Wealth built on exploitation is fragile. Laban's estate thrived temporarily, but his refusal to honor Jacob eventually cost him a generational inheritance.

2. Relationships matter more than resources. Laban saw Jacob as labor, not legacy. In contrast, Jacob became the father of Israel.

3. Don't confuse control with covenant. Laban tried to control outcomes, but covenant rests on faith and obedience, not manipulation.

4. God blesses the oppressed. Jacob, despite being under Laban's thumb, left Haran exceedingly rich.

5. Short-term profit leads to long-term loss. Laban lost the favor, flocks, and future that could have been his had he honored his agreement.

6. Manipulation invites divine correction. God warned Laban in a dream not to harm Jacob, proof that divine justice defends the exploited.

7. You can't hijack someone else's blessing. Laban tried to benefit from Jacob's grace without respecting the source.

8. Dishonest gain leads to broken families. Laban's daughters, Rachel and Leah, eventually turned against him, affirming Jacob's grievances.

The Great Departure: Loss Through Greed

When Jacob finally left Laban, he did so secretly, taking his wives, children, servants, and livestock. This wasn't just a family departure; it was an economic exodus. Jacob didn't just walk away; he took the future of Laban's wealth with him.

Laban pursued Jacob in anger, but God intervened in a dream, saying: *"Be careful not to say anything to Jacob, either good or* bad" (*Genesis 31:24*). The very God Laban had ignored now stood as Jacob's defense.

When they finally met, Jacob rebuked Laban: *"These twenty years I have been in your house… you changed my wages ten times… if the God of my father had not been with me, you would surely have sent me away empty-handed"* (*Genesis 31:38–42*).

This moment marks the collapse of Laban's empire. The wealth he had amassed began to dwindle. His daughters were gone. His grandchildren were gone. His livestock, the ones blessed by God, were gone. Laban's legacy ended in relational breakdown and financial depletion.

The Opportunist's Legacy

Laban's story is the antithesis of Abraham's. Where Abraham gave, Laban took. Where Abraham built altars, Laban built fences. Where Abraham blessed others, Laban controlled others. And yet, his story is preserved in Scripture for a reason: to warn, to instruct, and to remind us that wealth without worship is dangerous.

If Laban had honored Jacob, partnered with him, and acknowledged God's role in the blessing, he could have become a patriarchal partner in destiny. Instead, he became a symbol of short-sighted wealth, a man who won every deal but lost his destiny.

Final Thoughts: When Profit Replaces Principle

Laban's wealth was real, but not righteous. He teaches us that the ends never justify the means in kingdom economics. Even if your balance sheet grows, if your methods are corrupt, your legacy will crumble.

He is the modern picture of those who exploit labor, manipulate deals, and sacrifice people for profits. But he also reminds us that God watches, and divine justice eventually tilts the scales.

In the end, the blessed man walked away wealthy, and the wealthy man walked away alone.

Let Laban's life be a mirror and a message: choose legacy over leverage, covenant over control, and righteousness over riches.

"When wealth becomes empire and empire becomes god, fortunes rise like pyramids, yet still crumble to dust."

CHAPTER 16

The Pharaohs of Egypt: Sovereigns of Surplus

Estimated Wealth: $1 Trillion

In the grand tapestry of biblical wealth, no empire casts a shadow quite like ancient Egypt. At the center of that imperial affluence stood the Pharaohs, rulers whose influence extended from palaces to pyramids, from national grain banks to military conquests. While not always portrayed in a favorable light, Pharaohs were undeniably billionaire monarchs, managing national economies, international trade, monumental construction, and resource control at scales few could rival.

Unlike individual patriarchs who built wealth through flocks, fields, or divine favor, the Pharaohs represented institutional wealth, accumulated, consolidated, and wielded through central authority. Their power was economic, political, military, and spiritual, as they were viewed as gods among men. In biblical narratives, Egypt emerges not just as a backdrop of oppression but as a prototype of empire economics. This chapter explores how the Pharaohs of Egypt

[4]built and managed extraordinary wealth, the biblical moments that reveal their financial prowess, and the spiritual and economic principles that can be gleaned from their example, both positive and cautionary.

A Legacy of Centralized Wealth

Egypt's wealth predates many of the biblical figures already discussed. From the early dynasties onward, Pharaohs oversaw an economy dependent on the fertility of the Nile River, the labor of thousands, and the gold mines of Nubia. Egypt's economy was centrally planned. The Pharaoh was not just a ruler, he was the sole owner of the nation's land, the controller of its crops, and the manager of its military-industrial complex. By the time of *Abraham (Genesis 12)*, Egypt was already wealthy enough to be a place of refuge during famine. Abraham himself benefited from the generosity, or fear, of Pharaoh, receiving sheep, oxen, donkeys, male and female servants, and camels (*Genesis 12:16*).

This initial encounter sets the stage: Egypt was a land of wealth, capable of absorbing foreign travelers and sustaining millions. The Pharaohs did not simply sit on their wealth, they controlled

---

[4] Historical records of the Persian Empire under Xerxes I indicate vast royal wealth, yet Queen Vashti's legacy rests not in riches but in her bold stand for dignity and principle (Esther 1:9–12).

agriculture, taxation, and labor in ways that mirrored the world's first true economic superpower.

Joseph and the Pharaoh's Economic Empire

The clearest biblical window into Egyptian wealth strategy appears during the time of *Joseph*, who rose from prisoner to prime minister under a Pharaoh who was both discerning and strategic. *Genesis 41* records Pharaoh's dream of seven fat cows and seven lean cows, interpreted by Joseph as seven years of abundance followed by seven years of famine. Pharaoh empowered Joseph to create a national economic plan, the first of its kind. Joseph taxed 20 percent of the produce during the years of abundance and stored it in vast granaries. When famine came, Egypt became the only nation with food. The result was nothing short of a governmental wealth transfer:

1. The people first paid with money (*Genesis 47:14*).

2. Then with livestock (*Genesis 47:17*).

3. Then with land (*Genesis 47:20*).

4. Finally, they sold themselves into service (*Genesis 47:21*).

This process made Pharaoh the sole owner of virtually everything in Egypt. What began as stewardship ended in complete state control. Pharaoh's wealth was now not only agricultural or monetary but territorial and human. Pharaoh's cooperation with Joseph shows that wise leadership listens to prophetic insight. His wealth was protected because he acted on divine revelation, even though he was not a Hebrew believer.

Monumental Wealth in Monumental Projects

Pharaohs expressed their wealth not only through economy but through engineering. The pyramids of Giza, the temples of Karnak, and the lavish tombs of the Valley of the Kings were not just religious expressions, they were economic statements. These massive projects employed thousands of workers, artisans, and scribes, often for decades. Egypt's ability to mobilize labor at scale, fund architecture, and sustain cities around these projects proved their extraordinary treasury systems. Temples were centers of grain storage, libraries, banking, and taxation. The priests operated as administrators of both religion and economic life. In *Exodus 1:11*, we learn that the Israelites were forced to build the store cities of Pithom and Rameses, further evidence of Pharaoh's strategy of expanding storage and resource hubs. Pharaoh's strength came from preparation; he built to contain the surplus before the crisis came.

When Wealth Becomes Oppression

The darker side of Pharaoh's affluence appears in *Exodus*. As a new king arose "who knew not Joseph," he feared the population growth of the Israelites and turned them into slaves (*Exodus 1:8–14*). This marks the transformation of wealth from benevolence to bondage. Pharaoh enslaved the Hebrews not because of crime or rebellion but because of fear of losing control over wealth and power. He equated prosperity with permanence, failing to realize that oppression often brings judgment. Egypt's economy, once blessed through Joseph's prophetic leadership, became sustained by forced labor, economic injustice, and exploitation. Pharaoh is warned multiple times through Moses, but his heart remains hard. He sacrifices human rights to protect national wealth. This shift teaches us that prosperity without morality becomes tyranny. Pharaoh represents governments or leaders who accumulate power and possessions at the expense of ethics.

Divine Disruption: Wealth Under Judgment

In *Exodus 7–12*, Egypt is rocked by ten plagues, each one dismantling an economic structure:

1. Water to blood, agriculture and trade collapse.

2. Frogs, lice, flies, hygiene and public systems fail.

3. Livestock disease, food and transport disrupted.

4. Boils, public health crisis.

5. Hail and locusts, crops and wealth vanish.

6. Darkness, symbolic end of spiritual and economic rule.

7. Death of firstborn, national grief and succession crisis.

These were not random events, they were economic plagues, targeting Egypt's pride and possessions. God demonstrated that no empire is above divine accountability. When Israel finally departed, they *plundered the Egyptians* (*Exodus 12:36*). The wealth of Egypt was transferred to former slaves, proof that wealth can shift by divine decree, not just market mechanics.

Wealth Lessons from the Pharaohs of Egypt

1. Systematize surplus, Pharaoh's 20 percent tax during prosperity ensured survival.

2. Listen to prophetic voices, Pharaoh prospered when he heeded Joseph.

3. Build infrastructure, cities, storehouses, and agriculture were strategic.

4. Power is not eternal, hard hearts attract judgment.

5. Slavery corrodes success, economies built on injustice cannot endure.

6. Transfer of wealth is possible, what was hoarded by Egypt was inherited by Israel.

7. Use power to serve, not subjugate, Pharaoh could have used wealth to bless all peoples.

8. Recognize the source, Egypt forgot that God's favor was the reason for their rise.

Final Thoughts: Empire Without Eternity

The Pharaohs of Egypt embodied an unmatched blend of wealth, power, and architectural legacy. Yet none of their treasure, tombs, or tyranny could save them from divine judgment. They teach us that even the greatest institutions of man can be shaken when they oppose the purposes of God. While Pharaohs were billionaires by every measure, their legacy reminds us: without righteousness, wealth becomes a weapon; without humility, power becomes a pitfall. The Pharaohs rose by wisdom and fell by pride. In the economy of God, obedience always outweighs opulence.

"He had everything money could buy, yet walked away empty, because what he lacked could never be purchased."

CHAPTER 17

The Rich Young Ruler: When Wealth Meets a Wounded Will

Estimated Wealth: $20 Billion

In the Gospels, there is one man whose name we never learn, but whose wealth, potential, and tragic decision echo through time. Known only as the Rich Young Ruler, he appears in all three Synoptic Gospels (*Matthew 19:16–30, Mark 10:17–31, Luke 18:18–30*). Though he never becomes a patriarch, prophet, or king, his encounter with Jesus reveals one of the most profound lessons on wealth and discipleship in all of Scripture. This chapter examines his story not to shame him, but to extract wisdom.

The Rich Young Ruler is the perfect case study for how good intentions, religious behavior, and wealth alone are not enough for a kingdom legacy. In fact, he teaches us that having possessions is not the problem, but when possessions have us, the cost is eternal.

1. A Promising Profile

The Rich Young Ruler had every external advantage. He was young, which suggested energy, opportunity, and future. He was a ruler, implying political or religious influence. And he was rich, signifying financial success and material stability. In today's language, he would be a tech startup founder, a social media influencer, or a young real estate mogul. He had what many chase: money, youth, and authority. But he was still empty. He came running to Jesus, not casually walking but running, indicating urgency. His question? *"Good Teacher, what must I do to inherit eternal life?"* (*Mark 10:17*). His heart, though burdened by wealth, still longed for eternity. And that longing set the stage for a moment of divine opportunity and divine test.

2. The Heart Behind the Inquiry

On the surface, the question sounds noble. But Jesus quickly detects something deeper. He first challenges the ruler's use of the word *"good,"* redirecting attention back to God as the source of moral authority. Then Jesus quotes the commandments: *"You shall not murder, you shall not commit adultery, you shall not steal..."* and so on. The young man replies confidently: *"All these I have kept since my youth."* His religion was clean. His résumé was polished. But obedience without surrender is still control. He was moral, but not yielding. He followed the rules, but he was not following the Person of the Kingdom. Jesus looked at him, loved him, and offered a transaction far more costly than money: *"Go, sell all you have and give to the poor, and you will have treasure in heaven. Then come, follow Me"* (*Mark 10:21*). This was not a punishment; it was a promotion.

3. The Divine Investment Opportunity

Jesus did not just ask him to sell everything. He invited him to invest eternally: *"and you will have treasure in heaven."* The invitation was to exchange temporary wealth for eternal significance. He could have become the 13th disciple. His name could have been known like Peter, James, or John. Instead, he walked away. Why? Because *"he had great wealth."* His grip on money was stronger than his grasp on destiny. He failed the test every kingdom investor must pass: Will you lay it down when God calls for it?

4. Lessons from a Missed Moment

This young ruler teaches us more in his failure than many do in their success. Below are vital lessons modern wealth builders must not ignore:

a) Success without surrender is still a dead end. You can be religious, respected, and wealthy, and still miss the Kingdom. Jesus did not reject his wealth; He revealed the ruler's idolatry. When anything becomes untouchable by God, it becomes a barrier to destiny.

b) Wealth is a tool, not a trophy. This ruler treated wealth as a badge of righteousness. But Jesus challenged him to redistribute it for a purpose, not display. Kingdom capitalists see money as fuel, not furniture.

c) Following Christ may cost earthly comforts. Jesus does not always require the selling of assets, but He always involves the surrender of control. For this ruler, wealth was not the issue; ownership was.

5. What If He Had Said Yes?

Imagine with me: what if the Rich Young Ruler had said yes?

- He would have sat at the feet of the Messiah.

- He may have replaced Judas as treasurer or become the financier of the early church.

- His wealth could have built schools, fed the poor, or funded Paul's missionary journeys.

- His story could have ended with eternal rewards, not earthly regret.

This shows us that wealth in the wrong hands dies with the man, but wealth surrendered to the Master lives forever.

6. Modern Applications: Wealth at the Altar

Many believers today stand where the Rich Young Ruler stood, on the edge of full surrender. God may not be asking you to liquidate your assets, but He may be asking you to:

- Let go of selfish ambitions.
- Use your profits to fund missions.
- Say no to a lucrative but unethical deal.
- Invest in a kingdom project that yields no earthly ROI.

The Rich Young Ruler reminds us that delayed obedience is disobedience, and indecision is a decision.

7. Spiritual Warfare Over Wealth

There is a reason why the ruler's test came right at the door of eternal life: money is spiritual. It is not neutral. It has power, influence, and potential to either magnify God or glorify man. Satan fights hardest in the area of wealth because whoever controls wealth controls influence. That is why Jesus said, *"You cannot serve both God and mammon"* (*Matthew 6:24*).

The Rich Young Ruler was not just facing a test of generosity; he was facing a warfare of allegiance.

8. The Wealth That Follows Sacrifice

In response to the ruler's departure, Peter said, *"We've left everything to follow You."* Jesus replied with a promise for every obedient believer: *"Truly I tell you... no one who has left home or brothers or sisters or mother or father or children or fields for Me and the gospel will fail to receive a hundred times as much in this present age... and in the age to come eternal life"* (*Mark 10:29-30*). This is not poverty theology. It is priority theology. God does not want your riches; He wants your rule over riches submitted to Him.

Final Thoughts: Don't Just Run to Jesus, Follow Him

The Rich Young Ruler ran to Jesus, but stopped short of surrender. He knelt in reverence, but he would not rise in obedience. His story is a mirror to our modern world: talented, resourced, religious, but unwilling to release. But your story can be different. Let go. Surrender. Invest eternally. Build modern wealth with ancient wisdom. And when Jesus calls, may you not walk away sorrowfully, but rise wealthy, willing, and radically obedient.

CHAPTER 18

Queen Vashti: The Billion-Dollar Boundary

Estimated Wealth: $20 Billion

She was a queen draped in majesty, commanding the admiration of an empire that stretched from India to Ethiopia. Her name was *Vashti*, and although her story is often told as a mere footnote to Queen Esther's rise, it deserves deeper examination. Far from being just a rebellious wife, Queen Vashti was a woman of dignity, courage, and immense wealth. Historical and economic assessments of the Persian Empire during the time of *Ahasuerus* (*Xerxes I*) suggest that Vashti, as his queen, had direct access to influence and material wealth exceeding $20 billion in modern value. But Vashti's story is not just about opulence. It is about principles, boundaries, and the cost of dignity in a world where power is often abused.

This chapter explores how wealth, when joined with self-respect, can become a symbol of strength, even when it leads to personal sacrifice.

1. Wealth in the Palace of Power

The book of *Esther* opens with a grand feast that showcases the unimaginable wealth of the Persian Empire. King Ahasuerus ruled over 127 provinces, and his kingdom was the largest and most prosperous on earth at the time. Gold cups, marble pillars, luxurious drapes, and silver couches decorated the setting. The extravagance was deliberate, meant to project power, influence, and unmatched splendor (*Esther 1:1–7*).

Vashti was not merely an ornamental queen; she was part of this imperial machinery. She presided over her own banquet for the women of the palace, a role that indicated authority, prestige, and autonomy. Her wealth was not only monetary; it was political and cultural. In a world dominated by male hierarchy, Vashti stood tall as a woman of position and wealth in her own right.

Estimated Net Worth: Adjusting for the Persian Empire's global reach, gold reserves, and tribute system, Vashti's personal wealth, dowries, jewels, and royal privileges are conservatively estimated at $20 billion in modern value.

2. The Queen's Defiance: A Pricey Refusal

When King Ahasuerus summoned Vashti to parade her beauty before drunken nobles, she refused. It was not a refusal based on pride, but on principle. She understood her worth and would not allow herself to be objectified, even by royal command.

This act of defiance cost her everything: her position, her influence, and the full privileges of her wealth. But what she gained in moral integrity remains unmatched, a legacy of boundary-setting, self-respect, and dignity in the face of exploitation.

In modern language, Vashti was a billionaire who said no to misogyny, even when it meant forfeiting the throne. She became the costliest *"no"* in biblical history, but also one of the most courageous.

3. The Strength of a Boundary

Vashti teaches a timeless principle: no amount of wealth can replace a clear conscience. She could have obeyed and retained her crown, her palace, and her comforts. But she chose the more challenging path.

That act echoes a vital wealth-building truth: your boundaries define your brand. Too many people sacrifice character on the altar of cash flow. Vashti chose to sacrifice opportunity on the altar of principle, and in doing so, she built an invisible empire of respect that generations still honor.

4. Wealth Lessons from Queen Vashti

Though Vashti's story is short in the biblical record, her life offers rich principles for modern billionaires, entrepreneurs, and marketplace leaders:

1. *Dignity is worth more than visibility.* Vashti had the world's spotlight, but she walked away from it to preserve her dignity. In an era of digital fame, this lesson reminds us that integrity outlasts popularity.

2. *Boundaries build inner wealth.* True wealth is not just what is in your vault, but what is in your soul. Vashti's inner wealth, self-respect, courage, and moral clarity, was priceless.

3. *Every no makes room for a bigger yes.* Her refusal made room for Esther's assignment. Though Vashti lost her throne, she cleared the way for God's redemptive plan to unfold. Sometimes, your loss is another's gain, and that is kingdom orchestration.

4. *Women can be wealthy and principled.* Vashti was not weak, indecisive, or emotional. She was resolute, decisive, and dignified. She stands as a model for women who lead with clarity and conviction in high places.

5. Was She Rebellious or Revolutionary?

Many traditional interpretations label Vashti as insubordinate. But upon closer inspection, her action was one of ethical resistance. She refused to be humiliated, even if it meant royal backlash.

In today's marketplace, such courage is rare but needed. When CEOs, board members, or public figures bow to pressure at the cost of their values, they may retain status but forfeit legacy. Vashti's example reminds us that legacy is built on what you refuse, not just on what you achieve.

6. The Legacy of Hidden Reformers

We never read of Vashti again. Her name disappears after chapter one. But her influence lingers like a whisper in Esther's rise. Because Vashti said no, Esther could say yes. Because Vashti stood tall, another woman could stand chosen.

We often remember the names that finish, but we must also honor the ones who stood firm, even if they were written out of the narrative. Sometimes, reformers are hidden in history but immortalized in eternity.

7. Final Reflections: The Cost of Courage

Vashti reminds us that wealth without wisdom is dangerous, and wealth without boundaries is destructive. She risked everything to say no to objectification. And in doing so, she left a model for the modern world:

- CEOs with ethics
- Politicians with backbone
- Influencers with restraint
- Women who will not trade integrity for inclusion

Wealth should serve the soul, not suppress it. Vashti had both. And even when she lost her palace, she kept her power.

Closing Words: Be Like Vashti

Not every wealthy person ends their story in opulence. Some end it in obscurity, but with their dignity intact. Vashti may not have saved a nation like Esther, but she saved herself from disgrace, and in doing so, became a different kind of hero.

She reminds us that sometimes the most powerful thing you can do with your wealth, your position, and your influence is to say *no*.

CHAPTER 19

Nebuchadnezzar II: The Trillionaire Emperor of Earthly Glory

Estimated Wealth: $2.5 Trillion

At the height of his reign, *Nebuchadnezzar II*, King of Babylon, was the wealthiest, most powerful, and most architecturally ambitious ruler the world had ever seen. With an empire stretching from Egypt to Persia and from the Mediterranean Sea to the Persian Gulf, he not only commanded nations, he commanded awe. His wealth, when converted to today's values, is estimated at a staggering $2.5 trillion or more, making him arguably the wealthiest ruler in biblical history.

However, Nebuchadnezzar's story is not just one of unmatched affluence. His life serves as both a cautionary tale and a roadmap, a dramatic rise, a divine humbling, and a powerful restoration. This king-built empires, conquered continents, erected one of the *Seven Wonders of the Ancient World*, and yet ultimately bowed, not to any army, but to the authority of Almighty God. This chapter explores the vast wealth, leadership lessons, and spiritual insights embedded in the life of Nebuchadnezzar II, showing us how God speaks even to kings in palaces made of gold.

1. A Rise Like No Other

Nebuchadnezzar II reigned from approximately 605 to 562 BCE and transformed Babylon into the world's capital of innovation, splendor, and wealth. He inherited a powerful kingdom from his father, *Nabopolassar*. Still, he elevated it to unimaginable heights through military conquest (including the defeat of Assyria and Egypt), aggressive expansion of trade and tribute networks, and the enslavement of elite populations, including the Hebrews (*Daniel 1:3–4*).

Every victory brought gold, silver, exotic animals, enslaved people, spices, and materials into Babylon. His palace became a marvel, adorned with precious stones, carved cedar, and gold overlay. He spared no expense to ensure Babylon became the crown jewel of human achievement.

2. Estimated Wealth: Over $2.5 Trillion

Economists and historians estimate Nebuchadnezzar's empire collected tributes and trade revenues equivalent to over $2.5 trillion in today's terms. Consider the following components of his wealth:

- Gold-plated temples and idols, with Marduk's statue alone valued in tons of solid gold

- Control over key trade routes, taxing goods from Africa, India, and Asia

- The Hanging Gardens of Babylon, a legendary feat of architecture and hydraulics

- Massive storehouses of grain, livestock, weapons, and slaves

Nebuchadnezzar did not just collect wealth; he created a system of centralized economic control that generated endless revenue streams from dependent vassal states.

3. Babylon: The Billionaire's Playground

Under Nebuchadnezzar's leadership, Babylon became a global city of unparalleled magnificence. The *Ishtar Gate*, crafted with lapis lazuli and adorned with dragons and bulls, was one of the most ornate city entrances in ancient history. The walls of Babylon were so thick that chariot races could be held atop them.

The Hanging Gardens, one of the *Seven Wonders of the Ancient World*, symbolized his love for architectural dominance and his wife. This was not just wealth; it was a monument to human pride. Babylon was, by all human standards, unshakeable.

4. Lessons in Wealth Creation

Nebuchadnezzar mastered wealth creation through five strategic pillars:

a) *Dominate trade.* He controlled the fertile crescent's commercial arteries, allowing him to tax, transport, and trade nearly every valuable good known to man.

b) *Monopolize innovation.* Through urban development, irrigation, and engineering, he positioned Babylon as a hub of science and invention, drawing talent, artisans, and craftsmen globally.

c) *Harness forced labor.* While unethical, the system of enslaving conquered peoples enabled mass construction projects and wealth consolidation. The Hebrews were among those exiled to Babylon during this time.

d) *Leverage culture and religion.* He imposed the Babylonian language, names, education, and worship (as seen in *Daniel 1*), creating cultural dominance over subjugated peoples and securing loyalty and economic productivity.

e) *Invest in prestige architecture.* Monuments and marvels multiplied his legacy and reinforced his psychological grip on the empire.

In essence, Nebuchadnezzar treated wealth not just as currency but as a tool of control, glory, and identity.

5. The Dream That Shook a Billionaire

Despite his dominance, Nebuchadnezzar's real journey began with a troubling dream (*Daniel 2*). None of his magicians could interpret it; only Daniel, a Hebrew exile, gave the correct revelation: *"You, O king, are the head of gold."* (*Daniel 2:38*)

The dream warned of future kingdoms that would replace his, ending with God's eternal kingdom crushing all man-made empires. For the first time, Nebuchadnezzar saw that his trillions could not buy time, immortality, or spiritual security.

Still, he built a 90-foot golden image in defiance and demanded worship (*Daniel 3*). God responded with fire, literally. Moreover, though *Shadrach, Meshach, and Abednego* were thrown into it, they walked free, protected by a divine presence. God was not done with Nebuchadnezzar.

6. The Madness of a Trillionaire

In *Daniel 4*, Nebuchadnezzar had another dream, of a mighty tree being chopped down, symbolizing his own coming fall. Daniel warned him: *"Break off your sins by righteousness, and your iniquities by showing mercy to the poor"* (*Daniel 4:27*).

Twelve months later, the king stood on his rooftop and declared: *"Is not this great Babylon that I have built... by my mighty power and for the glory of my majesty?"* Immediately, a voice from heaven declared judgment.

Nebuchadnezzar lost his mind. He lived like a beast for seven years, eating grass, naked, and mentally broken. The world's richest man was reduced to a crawling symbol of pride's downfall. This was the bankruptcy of the soul.

7. The Restoration: Wealth Regained, Perspective Transformed

After seven years, Nebuchadnezzar lifted his eyes to heaven, and his sanity returned. Not just that, his kingdom, counselors, and wealth were restored. *"Now I, Nebuchadnezzar, praise and extol and honor the King of heaven... those who walk in pride He can abase."* (*Daniel 4:37*)

Here lies the greatest paradox of his story: he lost everything when he worshiped himself, but regained everything when he honored God. No other biblical billionaire experienced such a dramatic fall and restoration. God gave him a second chance, not just at rulership, but at reverence.

8. Spiritual and Financial Principles from a Trillionaire's Life

Nebuchadnezzar's journey is filled with essential lessons:

1. *Pride is a precursor to poverty.* He rose by strategy but fell by arrogance. His story reminds us that success without surrender is a setup for collapse.

2. *God rules above earth's richest.* Despite trillions in gold and silver, one word from heaven undid him. No matter your portfolio, God retains final authority.

3. *Restoration comes through recognition.* His wealth was restored only after he acknowledged God as sovereign. Restoration is not just about assets; it is about alignment.

4. *Your empire is temporary; God's Kingdom is eternal.* The most fabulous kings are those who realize their thrones are borrowed, their breath is God-given, and their riches must serve a higher purpose.

Final Reflections: The King Who Was Humbled

Nebuchadnezzar's story spans from opulence to madness, from dominion to deliverance. He was a man who touched the heights of human power but was not beyond the reach of divine discipline.

He teaches us that wealth without worship is hollow, and that the most valuable thing a ruler can possess is humility. His legacy is not in gold statues or wonder gardens; it is in the confession of a broken, restored man who finally saw that *heaven rules.*

"Her past was scandal, her present was courage, her future was redemption, and through faith, she became both wealthy and worthy."

CHAPTER 20

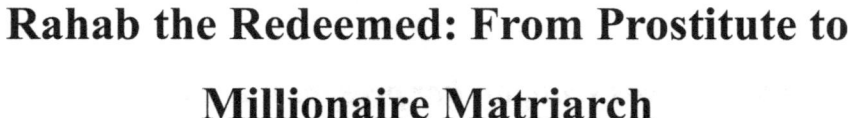

Rahab the Redeemed: From Prostitute to Millionaire Matriarch

Estimated Wealth: $5 Million

The name Rahab stirs curiosity, controversy, and ultimately a profound sense of awe. Known first in Scripture as a prostitute living in the pagan city of Jericho, Rahab's story is not one of material conquest like Solomon or Nebuchadnezzar. Instead, hers is a story of radical conversion, courageous faith, and remarkable elevation: a divine pivot that transformed a marginalized woman into a millionaire matriarch in the lineage of Christ. While she did not rule kingdoms or build temples, Rahab made a decision that changed history. Her wealth, estimated conservatively at $5 million in today's value, was likely accumulated through her high-ranking brothel, situated in a prime location on Jericho's city wall. However, the true wealth she gained came the day she traded her reputation for redemption.

This chapter explores how Rahab's bold faith, sacrificial courage, and strategic alignment with God's people ushered her into both material and eternal riches. Her story is proof that no past is too dirty for God to redeem, and no woman is too far gone to be repositioned for legacy-level wealth.

1. Rahab's House on the Wall: A Woman of Means

When the Israelite spies entered Jericho (*Joshua 2*), they went directly to Rahab's house. This was not by accident. Her establishment, built into the walls of the city, was strategically located for both visibility and escape, perfect for visitors, merchants, and yes, even espionage. Rahab was not a mere harlot on the street. She was a madam, a property owner, and a savvy businesswoman. Her house was her brand. Her clients ranged from soldiers to royalty.

Though immoral by spiritual standards, her business was lucrative. In the ancient world, high-ranking prostitutes were often well-connected, well-compensated, and socially shrewd. Based on ancient Near Eastern economies, Rahab's accumulated assets, property, gold, textiles, and influence, would likely place her modern-day net worth around $5 million.

2. The Risk That Birthed Her Redemption

Rahab's wealth, however, did not fulfill her. When the spies entered her home, something shifted. She recognized them not as customers, but as catalysts of God's judgment. Her words reveal the depth of her spiritual awakening: *"I know that the Lord has given you the land… for the Lord your God, He is God in heaven above and on the earth beneath"* (*Joshua 2:9,11*).

In that moment, Rahab switched kingdoms. She chose to risk her life, business, and future by hiding the spies. In return, she asked for mercy, for herself and her family. This act of faith and foresight positioned her for a miracle.

3. Faith Over Fortune: The Power of Her Conversion

Rahab's conversion was not ceremonial, it was radical. She left the gods of Jericho, the comforts of her wealth, and the protection of her city to identify with a foreign people and an unseen God. This was not just a spiritual decision. It was an economic sacrifice. She would soon leave her home, her assets, and her entire identity behind when Jericho fell.

However, the seed she planted, the scarlet cord in the window, became a prophetic symbol of her covenant with God. Her faith rewrote her future. *"By faith Rahab… did not perish with those who did not believe"* (*Hebrews 11:31*).

4. The Wealth of a New Life

When Jericho fell, Rahab was spared along with her household. However, God did not just save her. He repositioned her. She was brought into the camp of Israel and married Salmon, a nobleman from the tribe of Judah.

This union was not accidental. It was destiny. Rahab moved from prostitution to a partnership in royalty. Her husband was likely among the elite warriors or leaders in Israel, and together they became landowners and respected elders in the community.

Their son? Boaz, the righteous capitalist who married Ruth. Their lineage? King David. And then Jesus Christ.

Rahab's new life was not just saved; it was sown into a kingdom legacy. Her material prosperity, once rooted in sin, was now grounded in covenant. She became a matriarch of Messianic royalty, leaving behind a wealth that transcended gold.

5. Principles from a Redeemed Millionaire

Rahab teaches us that spiritual alignment can lead to financial and generational transformation. Her journey is full of life-changing lessons:

1. *Your past can be rewritten by faith.* She was once labeled a harlot, but heaven remembered her as a woman of faith. Your past does not seal your identity; your choices seal it.

2. *Faith requires sacrifice.* Rahab risked her safety and livelihood to align with God. Sometimes wealth God's way will cost you immediate comfort, but it leads to eternal gain.

3. *Courage is the gateway to covenant.* She did not wait passively, she acted decisively. Courage opens doors that money cannot.

4. *Alignment changes your assignment.* By aligning with the God of Israel, she stepped into an assignment far greater than her career. She became the womb through which generational wealth and salvation flowed.

5. *Redemption multiplies your value.* When God redeems you, He does not just clean you. He crowns you. He gave Rahab a new name, a new family, new wealth, and a new legacy.

6. The Hidden Power of the Scarlet Cord

The scarlet cord Rahab tied in her window is symbolic. It was not just a sign for the spies, it was a prophetic foreshadowing of the blood of Jesus, the ultimate sign of redemption. Through that bloodline, her name would be etched into *Matthew 1*, the genealogy of Christ.

This cord also represents:

- *A covenant:* God kept His promise to her.
- *A break from the past:* she left the old life behind.
- *A thread of redemption:* woven from Jericho to Jerusalem, from ruin to royalty.

7. Final Reflections: Rahab the Redeemed

Rahab's story reminds us that God's economy is upside down. He can take a scandalous woman from the edge of society and make her the cornerstone of a dynasty.

Her $5 million may pale in comparison to Solomon's trillions, but her wealth came not from conquest, but conversion. Not from manipulation, but mercy. She was not just a millionaire in potential; she was a millionaire in redemption.

God saw more than her past. He saw her prophetic future. Moreover, He wrote her name into the richest story ever told, the story of salvation.

CHAPTER 21

---※---

The Woman Who Touched the Hem: The Broken Millionaire Who Reached for Wholeness

Estimated Wealth: $5 Million

This affluent woman dedicated twelve long years to seeking a cure, depleting her substantial inheritance on relentless medical interventions. Her spending could be likened to a modern patient undergoing high-cost experimental treatments at premier institutions like Mayo Clinic, Johns Hopkins, and exclusive Swiss clinics, all at once. Historical context implies she pursued nearly every available healer from Jerusalem to Egypt, investing a fortune that, in today's terms, could underwrite the creation of an advanced medical research institute.

She is unnamed in the Gospel narrative, yet immortalized in the halls of faith. Her story is brief, but its impact is eternal. She did not come from a palace, nor did she command armies or trade routes. However, she held a different kind of wealth, one that had dwindled to nothing, chasing hope.

The woman with the issue of blood, as she is often called, began her journey as a woman of significant means, an estimated $5 million net worth in modern terms, but ended up destitute, desperate, and ostracized. However, her most incredible wealth was not what she once had, but what she reached for. In a single act of faith, she touched the hem of Jesus' garment and found what no amount of money could buy: healing, restoration, and wholeness.

This chapter examines the journey of this broken millionaire, a woman whose financial downfall was not due to folly but to the cost of survival. Her story reminds us that true wealth is found in faith and that even when all is lost, one touch from Jesus can restore everything.

1. A Woman of Substance and Suffering

Mark 5:25–26 tells us: *"And a certain woman, who had an issue of blood twelve years, and had suffered many things of many physicians, and had spent all that she had, and was nothing bettered, but rather grew worse..."*

This woman was not a beggar or ordinary peasant. The text implies that she had enough financial resources to seek out and pay for doctors for twelve consecutive years. In ancient Judea, medicine was costly, especially for ongoing, chronic conditions. The fact that she could sustain her medical pursuit for over a decade suggests she began with significant resources, likely inherited or earned through a family business or noble lineage.

Estimated Net Worth: Factoring in the economic standing of health-seeking women in Greco-Roman Judea, scholars suggest she could have held assets equivalent to approximately $5 million today; land, inheritance, livestock, textiles, jewelry, or managed trade.

She had wealth, yes. However, she also had a persistent hemorrhage, a medical and ceremonial affliction that cost her everything: her finances, her relationships, and her dignity.

2. Bankrupted by the System

In today's terms, this woman was like a cancer patient who had exhausted her insurance, savings, and assets on treatments that failed. She was exploited, disappointed, and isolated by religious law.

According to Levitical purity codes, her constant bleeding rendered her ritually unclean (*Leviticus 15:25–27*), meaning she could not enter the synagogue, she could not touch anyone without defiling them, and she likely lived alone, rejected by family and society.

Money could not buy her healing. It bought only false hope, and perhaps exploitation at the hands of physicians who used her desperation for gain. Her tragedy was not simply medical; it was economic, social, emotional, and spiritual. Her life was hemorrhaging on every level.

3. The Press Toward the Healer

The day she heard about Jesus was the day something shifted. She made her way through the crowd, not as a dignified patron, but as a woman in violation of ceremonial law, risking public shame or stoning.

She did not ask to speak to Jesus. She did not wait for permission. She reached for the hem of His garment: *"For she said, If I may touch but his clothes, I shall be whole."* (*Mark 5:28*)

This was not superstition. It was desperation drenched in faith. The hem of a Jewish rabbi's garment represented the fringes of the Law, the *tzitzit* that reminded Israel of God's commands (*Numbers 15:38–40*). She believed that His righteousness was greater than her uncleanness.

4. Instant Healing, Immediate Restoration

The moment she touched the hem; virtue flowed from Him and healing rushed into her body. Her bleeding stopped instantly. However, Jesus did more than heal her physically. He stopped and called her out publicly.

"Daughter, thy faith hath made thee whole; go in peace, and be whole of thy plague." (Mark 5:34)

This divine encounter did not just cure her; it reinstated her. Jesus publicly acknowledged her as *"daughter,"* granting her spiritual identity. He affirmed her faith, not her touch, as the key to healing. Moreover, he restored her place in society with his voice, not just his power.

She went bankrupt. She left blessed. Moreover, though Scripture does not detail her post-healing life, we can be certain she received more than health, she received purpose.

5. Wealth Lessons from a Bankrupted Believer

The woman who touched the hem teaches entrepreneurs, professionals, and investors that not all wealth loss is failure. Sometimes, losing everything positions you to gain what truly matters.

1. *Faith is the greatest currency.* She lost silver and gold, but what bought her healing was faith in action. In God's economy, faith moves what money cannot.

2. *Desperation is often the doorway to destiny.* Her desperation stripped her of pride and pushed her into destiny. When you

have nothing left but God, you are never more ready for a breakthrough.

3. *Systems may exploit, but God restores.* She suffered "many things from many physicians," but one encounter with Jesus restored twelve years of loss in a single moment. God's justice is redemptive.

4. *Your healing may come through courage.* She broke taboos, social norms, and religious barriers to touch Jesus. Many today miss their healing because they fear people more than they desire wholeness.

5. *Even the wealthy need Jesus.* She began as a wealthy woman. Her story reminds us that money cannot buy miracles, only faith can.

6. Final Reflections: The Touch That Transformed

This woman's journey is not just about bleeding; it is about breaking through. She bled in private, but her healing became public. She reached past shame, past trauma, past religion, and laid hold of grace.

Her story is for everyone who has ever spent their last dollar on things that did not work. For everyone who has walked through twelve years of waiting, rejection, and silent pain. She did not wait to be seen. She made her move. And heaven responded.

A Millionaire's True Reward

Though her wealth was lost in the pursuit of healing, she discovered a new kind of wealth: a relationship with the Son of God. That day, the woman who had once been a symbol of shame became a testimony of faith.

She teaches us that even when we hemorrhage financially, relationally, or emotionally, the hem of His garment is still within reach. Moreover, that one touch of faith can make us whole.

"In a world where power often corrupts, Cornelius showed that true greatness is found when wealth bows to worship and influence submits to God."

CHAPTER 22

Cornelius, God's Rich Marine

Estimated Wealth: $10 Million

In the bustling seaport city of Caesarea, one man stood out not only for his authority but for his authentic devotion. His name was Cornelius, a Roman centurion, an officer of elite military status. However, what made him exceptional was not his command over men; it was his sensitivity to God. He held both power and piety, and his wealth was matched only by his generosity and reverence.

Cornelius is often remembered as the first Gentile to receive the Holy Spirit in the New Testament, but beneath this spiritual milestone lies the compelling story of a wealthy, influential leader whose heart was deeply aligned with God's purposes. With an estimated modern net worth of around $10 million, Cornelius is the portrait of a Kingdom financier, a man who proved that you can be both affluent and anointed.

1. The Prestige of a Roman Centurion

To understand Cornelius's wealth and influence, we must first understand his position. A Roman centurion was the equivalent of a modern-day military commander, responsible for approximately 100 soldiers. They were highly trained, deeply respected, and well compensated by both military pay and civic perks. According to historical records, Roman centurions earned at least 15 to 20 times the salary of the average soldier. Additionally, they often received bonuses, land grants, property rights, and spoils from military campaigns. Over time, a loyal and successful centurion could accumulate enough wealth to purchase estates, invest in businesses, and even lend money.

Scholars and economic historians estimate that a centurion like Cornelius, stationed in a wealthy city like Caesarea, living in a coastal region with direct access to trade and commerce, could easily amass the equivalent of $10 million or more in today's terms, including property ownership in Roman colonies, tributes from subordinates, investment income from local businesses, and bonuses with imperial pensions.

2. A Generous Giver and God-Fearing Leader

Acts 10:2 describes Cornelius as: *"A devout man, and one that feared God with all his house, which gave much alms to the people, and prayed to God always."* Though a Gentile, Cornelius was spiritually awakened. He was not a casual seeker; he was a consistent giver. His life was marked by three defining traits:

reverence (he feared God even before full knowledge of the gospel), generosity (he gave much alms, not just spare change), and intercession (he prayed continually, developing a spiritual discipline rarely seen even among believers).

This combination of faith and finance made him Heaven's target. An angel appeared and said, *"Thy prayers and thine alms are come up for a memorial before God."* (*Acts 10:4*) This is profound: Cornelius' generosity had a spiritual echo. His giving reached God's throne. He was not just making donations; he was building memorials in the spirit.

3. Wealth That Heaven Recognized

Cornelius' wealth was not wasted on opulence or idleness. He used his resources to bless the poor, support the Jewish community, and raise a household in the fear of God. His faith shaped his finances, which in turn helped fund faith-based impact. This integrity, paired with economic power, positioned him as a social influencer respected by Jews and Romans alike, a Kingdom financier whose resources backed righteousness, and a spiritual bridge between two worlds, Gentile and Jew.

Moreover, when God needed a household through which to open the door to the Gentile world, He chose Cornelius. Not just because he prayed, but because he gave. He was a faithful steward, and stewards attract spiritual assignments.

4. The Day God Sent for Peter

Cornelius had a visitation. An angel told him to send for Simon Peter, who was staying in Joppa. Without hesitation, Cornelius deployed his resources and men, not to fight, but to receive revelation. He shifted his command from military matters to spiritual pursuits.

Peter, a Jew, entered Cornelius' home, a significant act since Jews avoided Gentile homes. However, the Holy Spirit was already orchestrating something historic. Cornelius had gathered his whole household and friends, ready to receive. Peter preached Jesus. And then, the Holy Spirit fell on the Gentiles, just as He had on the Jews at Pentecost. *"While Peter yet space these words, the Holy Ghost fell on all them which heard the word." (Acts 10:44)*

Cornelius was the first non-Jew to receive the Holy Spirit. His home became the launchpad of the global church's expansion to the nations. This is generational wealth at its highest; he birthed a new spiritual era.

5. Wealth Lessons from a Spirit-Filled Centurion

Cornelius teaches us that being a Spirit-filled believer does not require abandoning wealth; it requires redeeming its purpose.

1. True wealth serves God's purposes. Cornelius used his resources to give, serve, and host divine encounters. Wealth without mission is waste.

2. Generosity gets God's attention. His prayers and giving became a memorial, a fragrant offering before God. Generosity activates heavenly recognition.

3. Faith attracts visitation. His devout life positioned him for angelic and apostolic encounters. Some doors only open to faithful, generous people.

4. Kingdom wealth empowers households. Cornelius did not worship alone. His entire household was saved. He invested in the spiritual health of his home.

5. Wealth should bridge cultures. As a Roman, he reached across ethnic and religious lines. He used influence to unite people under the Gospel.

Cornelius was not merely a Roman military officer with wealth; he was a divinely positioned strategist whose faith, generosity, and spiritual sensitivity set in motion one of the most profound transitions in the early church: the opening of the Gospel to the Gentile world.

One afternoon, at the height of his devotion, Cornelius received a vision, not just a dream, but a supernatural encounter. An angel appeared to him, calling him by name and instructing him to send for Simon Peter. The precision of the angel's command underscores divine orchestration. Cornelius responded immediately, not out of obligation, but out of discernment. He recognized this was not ordinary; it was a summons from Heaven for a greater assignment.

Rather than keeping the experience private, Cornelius summoned his relatives and close friends to gather in his house. This was not simply curiosity or personal need for healing. He understood that what was coming was a moment of divine import, and he positioned his household to witness it. He created a spiritual platform for household revival. This was a man with both rank and revelation, one who combined military discipline with spiritual expectation.

As Peter arrived, reluctantly, having just come out of a vision where God corrected his Jewish exclusivity, Cornelius greeted him with humility, even falling at his feet. Peter lifted him, acknowledging their shared humanity, but the moment was charged with significance. Cornelius then opened his home, his heart, and his household to hear the word of the Lord. Moreover, as Peter preached the Gospel of Jesus Christ, the Holy Spirit fell on all who heard. It was Pentecost all over again, but this time, it fell on Gentiles.

In that moment, the Spirit of God validated that the Gospel was not limited by race, tradition, or national boundaries. Cornelius was not just a military man; he was a spiritual architect, a vessel used by God to pioneer the Gentile mission of the Gospel. His home became the prototype for Gentile churches. He had wealth, yes, but more than that, he had wisdom, influence, and the favor of God.

6. Final Reflections: The Centurion Heaven Could Trust

Cornelius was the type of man God could trust with both money and revelation. His $10 million wealth was not just in land or currency; it was in impact, influence, and eternal legacy. He became the gateway through which the Gentile world received the Gospel. Heaven knew his name. Earth respected his integrity. Moreover, the early church honored his obedience.

In a world where wealth often hardens hearts, Cornelius softened his before the Lord, and history changed because of it.

"Sometimes the greatest breakthroughs in history don't happen in palaces or temples, but in the ordinary homes of those willing to host God's interruptions."

CHAPTER 23

Simon the Tanner, The Millionaire Host of Divine Interruptions

Estimated Wealth: $30 Million

In the quiet coastal city of Joppa lived a man briefly mentioned in *Acts*, yet whose influence echoed through one of the most pivotal moments in church history. Simon the Tanner may not have held a royal title or commanded a military division, but he was a man of both substantial wealth and immense spiritual value.

As a tanner by trade, he worked with animal hides, converting raw skins into fine leather, a material in high demand for Roman military gear, scrolls, sandals, and luxury goods. Though the job was ceremonially unclean by Jewish standards, Simon occupied a vital niche in the Roman economy. With business rooted in international trade and contracts with soldiers, officials, and merchants, Simon's industry gave him an estimated modern-day wealth of over $30 million.

But Simon's value was not only in his profits; it was in his hospitality, humility, and alignment with God's purpose. Despite the

⁵social stigma attached to his occupation, he opened his home to one of the most prominent figures in the New Testament: Simon Peter, the lead apostle of Jesus Christ. This act, hosting a Jewish apostle in a ceremonially impure residence, reflected a powerful contradiction to religious norms. It showed that Simon was a man more concerned with divine alignment than societal approval. His house in Joppa became the setting for one of the most transformative visions in early Christianity: the revelation that the Gospel was meant for the Gentiles too.

Simon's success as a tanner meant he had a thriving operation, likely employing multiple workers, managing shipments across the Mediterranean, and conducting large-scale processing of hides. Leather was a foundational product in the first century, serving both functional and ceremonial purposes. From scrolls of Scripture to Roman armor and Jewish sandals, leather was everywhere. But tanning was dirty, odorous, and physically demanding work, involving lime, urine, and manure to cure the skins. Few wanted to be associated with it, but it was profitable. Simon carved out a high-value enterprise in a low-status industry, proving that purpose often hides in unlikely places.

---

⁵ *Though ceremonially unclean, the tanning trade was central to Roman commerce, providing leather for military and civic use; Simon's home later became the setting for Peter's transformative vision (Acts 9:43; 10:9–16).*

It was in this wealthy tanner's home that Peter stayed *"many days"* (*Acts 9:43*). This residence became the headquarters of transition. While resting on the rooftop, Peter fell into a trance and received a divine vision: a sheet descending from heaven filled with all kinds of animals, both clean and unclean. In that moment, God declared, *"Do not call anything impure that God has made clean."* This revelation dismantled Jewish exclusivity and opened the door for Gentiles to be included in the covenant of grace. But notice where it happened, not in a temple, palace, or synagogue, but in the home of a tanner, whose trade would have excluded him from mainstream religious circles.

By hosting Peter, Simon positioned himself at the crossroads of business, belief, and breakthrough. His home became a prophetic portal. His wealth became a platform for revelation. He gave Peter a place to rest, but more than that, he gave the Holy Spirit a place to speak. Without Simon's willingness to host Peter, the connection between Peter and Cornelius, the Roman centurion and first Gentile convert, might not have unfolded so seamlessly. The vision Peter received while in Joppa led directly to his journey to Caesarea, where he preached to Cornelius' household and witnessed the Holy Spirit fall on Gentiles for the first time.

There is no record of Simon preaching a sermon, working miracles, or traveling with the apostles. Yet his hospitality became holy. His business success enabled him to offer sanctuary to a man of God. His home, built by the rewards of craftsmanship and commerce, became the staging ground for the theological expansion of the early church.

Simon teaches us that wealth doesn't need to be flashy to be powerful. It doesn't need to be on public display to serve divine purpose. Sometimes, it's the quiet, grounded millionaire who provides the space for history to shift. His life reminds us that the Kingdom of God often advances not just through pulpits and platforms, but through homes and hospitality.

He also challenges our perception of vocation. Tanneries were despised by the religious elite, yet God chose a tanner's house as the setting for one of the greatest revelations of the Gospel age. This reminds us that no profession is too dirty, no space too humble, for the glory of God to descend. Simon's wealth was not only in currency, but in his courage to welcome God's messengers, even when it cost him social reputation.

Finally, Simon represents a new kind of entrepreneur: the Kingdom-aligned businessman. His resources, though vast, were secondary to his heart. His hospitality wasn't transactional; it was transformational. He didn't just build a tannery; he built a bridge for the Gospel to pass into new territory.

In the story of Simon the Tanner, we learn that wealth, when yielded to divine timing and purpose, becomes a vessel for revelation. He reminds us that the greatest investments we make may not be in portfolios or properties, but in people and obedience. And sometimes, the most powerful breakthroughs of the Kingdom happen not in cathedrals, but in tanneries, among the faithful who open their doors to God's servants and His agenda.

"Mary teaches us that the highest use of wealth is not preservation, but consecration, when treasure touches the feet of eternity."

CHAPTER 24

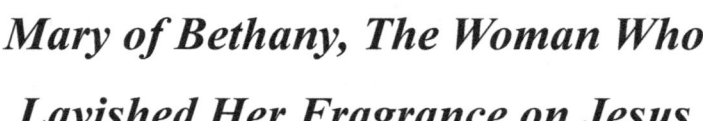

Mary of Bethany, The Woman Who Lavished Her Fragrance on Jesus

Estimated Wealth: $45 Million

In a world ruled by emperors and warriors, Mary of Bethany rose to prominence not with a sword or throne, but with a flask of perfume and a heart of unshakable devotion. Her wealth was evident, but her wisdom, rarer still, set her apart. She was no ordinary woman; Mary was a spiritual visionary, a prophetic worshiper, and an economic force whose estimated fortune today would be valued at over $45 million. However, she poured out her most prized possession, not into an investment portfolio, but over the dusty feet of the Son of God.

The Bible gives us glimpses into Mary's extraordinary character. She was part of a prosperous family alongside her siblings, Lazarus and Martha. Their estate in Bethany, a prestigious village near Jerusalem, hosted Jesus and His disciples, a sign of both their influence and affluence. Lazarus's burial in a private rock-hewn tomb further confirms their elite status. In an economy where property, livestock, and trade determined wealth, Mary's household held prime land, employed servants, and operated with the dignity of nobility. However, her true legacy would not be measured in acreage, but in the scent of her surrender.

The day Mary broke her alabaster jar of pure spikenard marked a defining moment, not only in her life, but in the entire redemption narrative. *Spikenard* was a rare, exotic ointment imported from the Himalayan regions of India. In today's terms, the value of her gift equaled hundreds of thousands of dollars, more than the annual wage of an upper-class worker. This was not perfume for display; it was an inheritance, a long-held treasure, possibly passed down through generations or reserved for her own burial. However, Mary offered it not to herself, but to the One she knew was worthy of everything.

As Jesus reclined at the table in her home, surrounded by men who misunderstood both His mission and her moment, Mary did what no one else dared to do. She shattered the seal of her alabaster flask and anointed His feet, wiping them tenderly with her hair. This was no emotional whim; it was a spiritual statement. She was embalming the Messiah before His death, prophetically preparing the body of Jesus before His final sacrifice. The fragrance filled the house, but more than that, it filled the silence of spiritual dullness with the sound of pure worship.

Others saw waste. Jesus saw wisdom. While the disciples; especially Judas, muttered about the value of the perfume, Mary made a transaction of eternal significance. She took what others might invest in properties or profits and deposited it into the Kingdom's most excellent offering, Christ Himself. Jesus responded with words that immortalized her act: *"She has done what she could... Wherever the gospel is preached throughout the world, what she has done will also be told, in memory of her."* No other person, male or female, was given such a promise from the Savior's lips. In that moment, Mary was crowned with eternal remembrance.

Mary of Bethany was not just generous, she was strategic, discerning, and deeply prophetic. She understood timing in the Spirit. While others were still trying to crown Jesus as a political king, she perceived that He was a suffering servant on His way to the cross. Her act of worship carried the weight of revelation. She poured out her perfume with the knowledge that death was coming, and glory would follow. This insight did not come from theological training but from sitting at the Master's feet, listening, absorbing, and worshiping. She anointed the Redeemer before redemption unfolded.

Her act challenges every person of influence and affluence. In a culture where net worth often speaks louder than spiritual worth, Mary reminds us that the most incredible wealth is the ability to give it all in worship. She held nothing back, neither her assets nor her affection. Her perfume was expensive, yes, but it became priceless the moment it touched the skin of God.

It is also worth noting that Mary had seen Jesus conquer death. She watched Him weep at Lazarus's tomb. She witnessed her brother walk out alive at Christ's command. She knew resurrection was not a theory, it was power in motion.

So, when she poured out the spikenard, it was not mere gratitude, it was honor from someone who knew Jesus not only as Teacher, but as *the Resurrection and the Life.*

From an economic standpoint, Mary's act would baffle any modern investor. Giving away what could be worth nearly half a million dollars in one sitting seems irrational. However, Mary was not investing in stocks, she was investing in eternal fragrance. Her oil became incense in the courts of Heaven. Her story became inseparable from the Gospel itself. Her action triggered a revelation that worship is not measured by volume, but by value.

Mary of Bethany teaches us that some offerings are so weighty they become prophetic events. Her perfume did more than prepare Jesus' body, it consecrated her name into divine history. She did not seek applause, but her act drew Heaven's recognition. Her home, once a quiet village estate, became the location of one of Scripture's most extravagant acts of worship.

Today, Mary stands as a rebuke to the cautious giver and a mentor to the radical worshiper. She is the woman who saw redemption walk into her house and responded not with words, but with a broken jar. Her story compels every reader to ask: *What treasure have I yet to break open at His feet? What revelation do I miss by playing it safe? What fragrance lies sealed in my alabaster box?*

Mary of Bethany, the $45 million woman, reminds us that the highest value of wealth is realized only when it is released in worship. Moreover, in her fragrance, we smell the beginnings of Calvary.

"Philemon's fortune was not measured by possessions kept, but by a house opened, a church sustained, and a legacy of reconciliation secured."

CHAPTER 25

Philemon, Millionaire Financier of Ministry

Estimated Wealth: $40 Million

In the bustling city of Colossae, known for its vibrant trade routes and textile commerce, lived a man whose faith was as rich as his fortune. Philemon, a prominent businessman and landowner, was not only known for his immense wealth, estimated today at over $40 million, but also for his generous spirit and his crucial role in the growth of the early church. His name, though recorded only once in the New Testament, stands as a testament to how kingdom-minded wealth can fuel both ministry and reconciliation.

Philemon's estate was no ordinary residence. It was expansive enough to serve as a meeting place for an entire congregation. In a time when Christian worship was banned from public temples and forums, Philemon opened his private home as a sanctuary. His wealth funded a house church, likely accommodating dozens of believers, providing not only shelter but also security, food, and spiritual nourishment. While others guarded their fortunes, Philemon offered his household as a platform for divine work.

But what sets Philemon apart in biblical history isn't just his money, it's how he used it to serve God's mission and Paul's ministry. Paul, the Apostle to the Gentiles, calls him *"our dear friend and fellow worker"* in the opening of the epistle bearing Philemon's name. That wasn't casual praise, it was a recognition of deep partnership, one forged not only through faith but also through sacrificial financial support and active involvement in building the church.

Philemon's influence extended beyond economics. He was a spiritual leader, a trusted host, and a man of strong ethical standing in a society often torn by class divisions and slavery. Yet his wealth did not separate him from the broken. In fact, the heart of his story is one of radical forgiveness and personal transformation. When his runaway slave, Onesimus, encountered Paul in prison and became a believer, it created a powerful moment of tension and redemption. Legally, Philemon had the right to punish Onesimus harshly. But Paul, knowing Philemon's character, appealed to him not as an apostle commanding obedience, but as a brother entreating mercy.

In his famous letter, Paul asks Philemon to receive Onesimus not as a slave but as *"a beloved brother."* This was a countercultural act, one that went against Roman law and social norms. For a man of

Philemon's stature to embrace a former servant as family would have been unthinkable. Yet Paul trusted that Philemon's understanding of grace, generosity, and love would override pride and property rights. This single act had the power to redefine relationships in the early church, illustrating that in Christ, there is neither slave nor free.

Philemon's decision would set a precedent for how wealthy believers should engage in the ministry of reconciliation. His willingness to forgive, to restore, and to release demonstrated that true kingdom wealth isn't hoarded, it's used to heal. He wasn't just a donor to Paul's ministry, he was a co-laborer in the gospel, someone whose financial strength was matched by spiritual maturity.

From a marketplace perspective, Philemon was the epitome of a successful first-century businessman. He likely traded in textiles, dyes, or agricultural goods, considering Colossae's proximity to Laodicea and its famous wool industry. His home likely served as both a commercial and spiritual hub, a place where commerce met conviction, and where transactions occurred not only in goods but also in grace.

Philemon also reflects the power of personal influence. His wealth gave him a voice in the community, but it was his faith that gave his voice authority. When he welcomed the church into his house, he wasn't simply allowing them to gather, he was making a public statement that his allegiance was with Christ, no matter the cost. That kind of open association with the faith, especially in the early days of persecution, was as courageous as it was costly.

In many ways, Philemon is a prototype of the Kingdom financier, a believer whose resources advanced the church, whose faith guided his leadership, and whose love produced visible fruit. His letter may be short, but the implications of his actions span generations. He teaches us that reconciliation is richer than revenge, that forgiveness is a more powerful investment than wealth, and that hospitality is holy when it opens the door for healing.

What would have become of Onesimus had Philemon not extended mercy? And how many more lives did that act influence? Church tradition holds that Onesimus later became a bishop, leading many to Christ. That chain of events started not in a synagogue, not in a revival, but in the heart of a wealthy man who decided to use his influence for redemption.

Philemon's story invites modern millionaires to ask deeper questions: How is my wealth serving God's purposes? Am I only investing in what benefits me, or am I sowing into stories that set captives free? Am I willing to host, forgive, give, and restore in the name of Christ?

In the example of Philemon, we find more than a wealthy landowner. We discover a patron of peace, a steward of justice, and a vessel through which God redefined what wealth truly looks like. His life declares that no investment outperforms love, and no fortune is more powerful than one that builds bridges instead of walls.

"The blessing of the Lord, it maketh rich, and he addeth no sorrow with it." — Proverbs 10:22

CHAPTER 26

Kingdom Wealth Principles: Building Lasting Prosperity by Heaven's Laws

Throughout the Bible, we witness men and women who became wealthy through divine alignment, strategic stewardship, and moral integrity. From Abraham to the Proverbs 31 Woman, and even in contrast to opportunists like Laban or Pharaoh, one truth becomes clear: God is not against wealth; He is against wickedness. Wealth, when gained by Kingdom principles, is a tool for righteousness, expansion, and generational impact.

This chapter distills the economic and spiritual principles behind biblical billionaires. We are no longer just examining personalities; we are identifying patterns. These patterns are not suggestions; they are heaven's protocols for increase. Whether applied by individuals or nations, these principles transcend time, culture, and currency.

To understand Kingdom wealth is to recognize that God's economy is not subject to earthly inflation, market crashes, or political regimes. It is based on obedience, honor, generosity, diligence, and covenant alignment. The following principles are foundational truths seen across every story in this book. They are the blueprint for lasting prosperity in the Kingdom of God.

1. The Principle of Covenant Alignment

Every biblical billionaire was connected to God through a covenant. Abraham's wealth flowed from the promise God made to bless him (Genesis 12:1–3). David's kingdom expanded through his heart for God's presence. Even Joseph, who rose in Egypt, carried a covenant identity in a foreign land.

Covenant is not simply a contract; it's a relational alignment with heaven's agenda. Prosperity becomes a byproduct of walking in God's will.

Application: Seek first the Kingdom (Matthew 6:33). Wealth is safest in the hands of those whose hearts are aligned with God's purposes.

2. The Principle of Purposeful Wealth

Biblical wealth always had a mission. Abraham used his riches to secure land. Solomon built a temple. Joseph used wealth to preserve a nation. Lydia used her enterprise to fund the early church.

Kingdom wealth is never about hoarding; it is about helping. Money is a servant, not a god.

Application: Before asking for an increase, define your Kingdom assignment. What will your money do for others, for God's work, and for future generations?

3. The Principle of Diligence and Skill

From the Proverbs 31 Woman to Jacob, from Boaz to Daniel, all were workers. They developed expertise, cultivated diligence, and solved problems. They didn't wait for handouts; they maximized what was in their hands.

Proverbs 10:4 declares, *"Lazy hands make for poverty, but diligent hands bring wealth."*

Application: Invest in mastery. Develop your gifts. Work with excellence. The Kingdom doesn't reward excuses, it honors execution.

4. The Principle of Generational Vision

Biblical wealth was generational. Abraham blessed Isaac. Isaac blessed Jacob. Jacob transferred the legacy to the twelve tribes. David prepared wealth for Solomon. A short-term vision produces fleeting wealth; a long view builds dynasties.

Proverbs 13:22 says, *"A good man leaves an inheritance to his children's children."*

Application: Think beyond yourself. Set up structures, trusts, education, business models, that outlast your lifetime.

5. The Principle of Divine Timing

Joseph stored grain for seven years. Isaac sowed during a famine. Solomon made treaties during peace. Timing isn't luck, it's spiritual discernment.

Ecclesiastes 3:1 reminds us, *"To everything there is a season..."* Kingdom billionaires don't just act, they discern.

Application: Don't move by emotion; move by revelation. Pray before investing. Ask God for timing before launching.

6. The Principle of Integrity

Job was wealthy not just because of what he had, but because of how he lived. Even Satan recognized Job's integrity. Daniel prospered under pagan kings because he refused to compromise.

Proverbs 11:3 says, *"The integrity of the upright guides them, but their duplicity destroys the unfaithful."*

Application: Your name is more valuable than your net worth. Protect your reputation. Operate in truth, even when it costs you.

7. The Principle of Radical Generosity

Abraham gave Melchizedek a tenth. David gave out of his own treasury to build the temple. The early church sold lands and distributed them to the poor. The wealthiest people in God's story were the most generous.

Luke 6:38 teaches, *"Give, and it will be given to you."*

Application: Make giving a lifestyle, not an event. Tithes, offerings, alms, these aren't charity gestures; they are Kingdom transactions.

8. The Principle of Wisdom

Solomon's wealth flowed from wisdom. He didn't ask for gold, he asked for understanding. As a result, he became the wealthiest man on earth.

Proverbs 8:18 says, *"With me are riches and honor, enduring wealth and prosperity."*

Application: Chase wisdom more than money. Read, learn, seek counsel, and pray for divine strategies.

9. The Principle of Prophetic Association

Many became wealthy due to their connections. Potiphar prospered because Joseph was in his house. The widow of Zarephath survived famine because she hosted Elijah. The Shunammite woman received a miraculous increase through Elisha.

Blessings often travel through relationships.

Application: Identify your prophetic alliances. Honor the men and women of God assigned to your destiny. Where there's grace, there's provision.

10. The Principle of Order and Stewardship

God never multiplies disorder. He had Noah build an ark according to precise measurements. He gave Moses the laws. Jesus multiplied fish and loaves, but had the people sit in groups of 50.

David set up treasuries and systems for temple construction. Joseph created storage systems. Nehemiah budgeted for the rebuild.

Application: Organize your finances. Budget, track, plan. Set goals. You can't steward millions if you mismanage hundreds.

11. The Principle of Strategic Investment

Isaac planted crops in famine and reaped a hundredfold. Solomon traded internationally. The Proverbs 31 Woman bought fields and invested in merchandise.

Kingdom wealth isn't mystical, it's strategic.

Application: Study markets. Diversify investments. Don't bury your talent, multiply it.

12. The Principle of Spiritual Warfare

Not every financial battle is natural. Satan attacked Job. Israel's prosperity provoked Egypt's oppression. Jesus was betrayed for silver.

Wealth attracts warfare.

Application: Pray over your business. Cover your assets. Bind devourers. Break curses of poverty and limitation.

13. The Principle of Legacy Leadership

David raised Solomon to build. Moses mentored Joshua. Jesus trained disciples. Kingdom wealth is sustained by multiplying leaders, not just accumulating assets.

Application: Build teams. Train successors. Share wisdom. Empower others to prosper.

14. The Principle of Divine Justice

God balances economies. The Israelites plundered the Egyptians. The wealth of the wicked is stored up for the righteous (Proverbs 13:22). He defends the poor and blesses the faithful.

Application: Don't chase corruption. God is your promoter. Your harvest is guaranteed, if your seed is righteous.

15. The Principle of Gratitude and Worship

David danced before the Lord with his whole heart. Abraham built altars. Solomon offered a thousand burnt offerings. Worship attracts wealth because it attracts God.

Application: Praise is a portal. Never let your prosperity outgrow your worship. Gratitude keeps your heart clean and your heavens open.

Final Thoughts: Building with Kingdom Blueprints

Kingdom wealth is not a lottery; it's a lifestyle. It is governed by divine laws, tested by time, and rewarded with legacy. The billionaires of the Bible weren't perfect, but they obeyed divine principles that produced supernatural results.

As this book has shown, the path to prosperity is paved with obedience, wisdom, work, and worship. True wealth isn't measured by what you have, but by what you've built, protected, and passed on in alignment with God's will.

Let your journey into Kingdom wealth begin, not with a craving for coins, but with a covenant commitment. That's where all treasure begins.

"True prosperity is not found in the tools of the age, but in timeless principles that turn wealth into worship and resources into redemption."

CHAPTER 27

Building Modern Wealth God's Way

In today's digital age of cryptocurrency, artificial intelligence, global marketplaces, and remote entrepreneurship, the pursuit of wealth has taken on new dimensions. But even with advances in finance and technology, the timeless question remains: How can I build wealth in a way that honors God?

The world offers many models of success, some built on manipulation, greed, and exploitation. Yet Scripture presents a radically different paradigm: one where wealth is not only gained but sanctified. In God's Kingdom, wealth is not merely accumulation; it is assignment. It is not about being rich for riches' sake, it is about becoming resourceful for redemptive purposes.

In this final chapter, we bridge the gap between ancient biblical wealth and contemporary financial opportunity.

We explore how believers can build modern wealth using eternal principles, ensuring that our prosperity reflects heaven's values.

1. Wealth Begins with Revelation, Not Just Education

While financial education is critical, understanding investments, budgeting, and asset building, Kingdom wealth begins with revelation.

Deuteronomy 8:18 reminds us: *"But you shall remember the LORD your God, for it is He who gives you power to get wealth."*

This power includes ideas, discernment, connections, and divine timing. God can drop a concept into your spirit that outperforms decades of market research. Biblical billionaires prospered because they heard from God, Joseph's grain storage plan, Solomon's wisdom, and Isaac's sowing in famine were all products of revelation.

Application: Prioritize time with God before you build. Ask for ideas, strategies, and spiritual clarity. Let God inspire your business model.

2. Embrace Industry with Integrity

In an era of side hustles, remote startups, and global outsourcing, the temptation to compromise for cash is real. But wealth God's way requires clean hands and a pure heart (**Psalm 24:3–5**).

Boaz prospered through fair treatment. Daniel thrived in government through honesty. Job was wealthy and blameless. In contrast, Gehazi and Ananias lost everything because of deception.

Application: Don't lie to scale faster. Don't exploit workers or cut corners. Choose righteousness over shortcuts. When your integrity is intact, God becomes your guarantor.

3. Leverage Technology, Guard Your Heart

Technology offers tools never available in Bible times, online platforms, passive income streams, blockchain, and more. But tools don't change character; they magnify it.

As technology expands our reach, our hearts must remain anchored. Jesus warned that a man's life does not consist in the abundance of possessions (**Luke 12:15**). Kingdom wealth is not about the volume in your vault but the virtue in your values.

Application: Use technology to serve others. Automate with wisdom. Build platforms with purpose. And regularly check: Is this building God's kingdom, or just my empire?

4. Build Wealth on the Foundation of Giving

God's economy is upside down: you gain by giving. Every biblical billionaire had a giving spirit. Abraham tithed. David gave for the temple. The Proverbs 31 Woman stretched her hand to the poor.

In contrast, the rich fool in **Luke 12** hoarded and died without a legacy. Kingdom wealth is not measured in accumulation, but in distribution.

Application: Tithe. Give to missions. Support widows. Fund scholarships. Set up legacy giving. You don't give because you're rich, you're rich because you give.

5. Invest in Multiple Streams

Ecclesiastes 11:2 says, *"Give a portion to seven, yes, to eight, for you do not know what disaster may come upon the land."*

This ancient advice echoes modern investment principles, diversify. Modern wealth builders should not depend on one income stream. Explore real estate, stocks, businesses, royalties, and intellectual property.

Application: Learn the markets. Get mentorship. Don't fear failure, steward risk wisely and prayerfully. Diversification protects legacy.

6. Operate in Kingdom Time

Timing is everything. Joseph stored grain before the famine. David waited to become king. Jesus waited 30 years to begin ministry.

Many lose wealth because they act out of impulse. Others delay until opportunity dies. Kingdom wealth requires discernment of divine timing.

Application: Pray before launching. Don't invest from FOMO (fear of missing out). Trust the Holy Spirit's leading, even if it doesn't look logical in the natural.

7. Build with Community, Not Isolation

The world teaches individualism: "Get yours." God teaches interdependence: *"Bear one another's burdens"* (**Galatians 6:2**). Kingdom wealth thrives in community ecosystems.

The early church pooled resources. Ruth gleaned with others. Nehemiah rebuilt with teams. Even Jesus chose disciples to spread the word.

Application: Collaborate. Share profits with partners. Mentor others. Wealth becomes meaningful when others rise with you.

8. Protect Your Mind from Poverty Strongholds

Poverty is not just the absence of money, it's a mindset. It includes fear, limitation, and small thinking. **Romans 12:2** urges us to be *"transformed by the renewing of your mind."*

Modern wealth requires mind renewal: rejecting scarcity, self-doubt, and shame. You must believe you are worthy of wealth and capable of managing it for God's glory.

Application: Declare prosperity promises. Read wealth-building Scripture. Listen to testimonies of Christian entrepreneurs. Break the agreement with generational poverty.

9. Don't Just Make Money, Multiply Meaning

Kingdom wealth is not just about net worth; it's about net impact. What legacy are you building? Are you solving problems? Elevating others? Expanding the gospel? Every dollar should be a disciple, going ahead to prepare the way for Kingdom influence.

Application: Build businesses that reflect God's values. Offer products and services that bring dignity. Use influence to uplift marginalized voices. Make your money matter.

10. Stay Humble as You Rise

Deuteronomy 8:17–18 warns: *"You may say to yourself, 'My power and the strength of my hands have produced this wealth for me,' but remember the Lord your God..."*

Pride is the silent killer of Kingdom wealth. Nebuchadnezzar lost everything until he acknowledged heaven. Lucifer was cast out for arrogance.

Application: Stay grounded. Give God credit publicly. Celebrate others' success. Be teachable. The higher you go, the lower you bow.

A New Breed of Billionaire

God is raising a new class of financial leaders, Kingdom billionaires who are as prayerful as they are profitable. They are strategic, yet surrendered. Bold, yet benevolent. They don't just want wealth; they want God's will funded.

You may never wear a crown like Solomon or build storehouses like Joseph. But if you walk in obedience, diligence, generosity, and integrity, you will prosper. And your prosperity will speak, not just of your brilliance, but of God's goodness.

This is how you build wealth in the modern world, God's way.

10 Powerful, Faith-Based Poverty-Breaking Decrees

Speak these daily to align your mind, spirit, and actions with biblical abundance and prosperity principles:

1. I decree that lack and insufficiency have no authority over my life; I walk in divine provision, overflow, and supernatural supply (**Philippians 4:19**).

2. I decree that I am a lender and not a borrower, the head and not the tail, above only and never beneath (**Deuteronomy 28:12-13**).

3. I decree that the blood of Jesus breaks every generational curse of poverty, debt, and financial delay; I inherit the wealth of the righteous.

4. I decree open doors of favor, increase, and opportunities are locating me now; divine ideas and resources are flowing into my hands.

5. I decree that the wealth of the wicked is being transferred into the hands of the righteous, and I am a steward of Kingdom wealth (**Proverbs 13:22**).

6. I decree that my hands are blessed; everything I touch prospers, and my storehouses overflow with abundance (**Psalm 1:3; Deuteronomy 28:8**).

7. I decree divine wisdom guides my financial decisions; I invest, build, and multiply resources according to God's strategies.

8. I decree that I break all agreements with a poverty mindset; I embrace abundance, productivity, and purpose-driven prosperity.

9. I decree supernatural cancellation of debt, release of withheld finances, and restoration of every financial loss.

10. I decree that I am blessed to be a blessing, my wealth shall fund the Gospel, rescue the hurting, and glorify God across the earth.

"The greatest legacy of wealth is not in what is stored on earth, but in how it advances the purposes of Heaven."

Conclusion: The Call of Kingdom Billionaires

We have journeyed through the corridors of time, walking beside kings, queens, prophets, warriors, entrepreneurs, and visionaries. We've heard the clink of coins in ancient treasuries, felt the rustle of royal robes in palace courts, and sensed the whispers of divine instruction spoken to the hearts of those who held the wealth of nations. But beyond the numbers, assets, and legacy estates, we've discovered something far greater, the divine blueprint for purpose-driven prosperity.

These were not just billionaires in bank balance; they were stewards of a sacred trust. Men and women like Abraham, Joseph, Mary of Bethany, and Philemon didn't merely accumulate wealth; they channeled it into causes that echoed into eternity. They funded temples, fed nations, rescued lineages, protected generations, and advanced the Gospel. Their wealth had a mission. Their success had stewardship. And their names were recorded, not in Forbes, but in the inspired pages of God's Word.

What makes their stories unforgettable is not merely their riches, but how they responded to the call of God in the marketplace. They remind us that faith is not meant to be divorced from finances. The

Kingdom of God does not advance on inspiration alone, it moves forward through those willing to risk, give, build, and release. God trusted them with treasure because He could trust them with vision.

You, too, stand at the edge of that same invitation.

Today, God is raising a new breed of billionaires, not for self-enrichment, but for Kingdom empowerment. You were not created to chase money, but to master it for the glory of God. You are not a beggar in the economy of Heaven, you are a builder, a distributor, a divine strategist in the unfolding plan of God for nations.

The world is in desperate need of righteous capitalists, men and women who are as generous as they are gifted, as prophetic as they are prosperous. The next great moves of God will be financed by those who understand that provision follows vision, and that divine wealth is entrusted, not just earned.

Let this book be your awakening. Let the stories of biblical billionaires stir your spirit, renew your goals, and ignite your courage. You have ideas inside you that can solve global problems. You carry favor that can open impossible doors. You walk with a God who owns the cattle on a thousand hills, and who longs to entrust wealth to those who walk in wisdom, humility, and fearless faith.

So, rise. Build. Invest. Forgive. Fund. Risk. Create.

Break the alabaster box, plant like Isaac. Negotiate like Jacob. Govern like Joseph. Worship like Mary. Give like Boaz, rule like David. Believe like Abraham.

The greatest fortunes are not measured in gold, but in impact, in obedience, in legacy.

You may never wear a crown like Solomon or command a treasury like Pharaoh, but if your wealth builds the Kingdom, redeems the broken, and glorifies God, then Heaven will call you rich indeed.

You were never meant just to read this book. You were born to live it.

Now go, and become a billionaire with a purpose.

Appendices

Appendix A: Wealth-Building Principles from the Billionaires of the Bible

Name	Estimated Worth	Key Wealth-Building Principle
Abraham	$100 billion+	Generational covenant wealth; obedience to divine call
Isaac	$50 billion	Wealth by inheritance, sowing, and supernatural return
Jacob	$80 billion	Strategic labor, divine encounter, and entrepreneurial skill
Joseph	$100 billion	Stewardship, vision, crisis management

Solomon	$2.2 trillion	Wisdom-driven abundance, global trade, kingdom investments
David	$1 billion+	Leadership, favor, and military conquest
Hezekiah	$30 billion	Wealth preservation, divine protection, national stewardship
Laban	$75 million	Opportunism, negotiation, family wealth leveraging
Pharaohs of Egypt	$1 trillion+	Empire control, resource storage, agriculture & taxation
Boaz	$120 million	Righteous capitalism, generational restoration
Rich Young Ruler	$100 million	Cautionary tale, wealth without surrender
Josiah	$6 billion	God-honoring reform, treasury restoration

Vashti	$20 billion	Royal legacy, female influence in palace economy
Nebuchadnezzar II	$2.5 trillion+	Imperial power, global dominion, humbling by God
Rahab the Prostitute	$5 million	Redemption, risk, and realignment to covenant
Woman with the Issue	$5 million	Exhausted wealth → divine healing and restored purpose
Cornelius	$5 million	Strategic generosity and gateway to Gentile evangelism
Simon the Tanner	$30 million	Businessman as host for apostolic movement
Mary of Bethany	$45 million	Lavish worship, prophetic giving
Philemon	$40 million	Ministry patronage, forgiveness, reconciliation leadership

Appendix B: 12 Kingdom Wealth-Building Lessons

1. **Worship before Wealth** – Mary of Bethany shows giving precedes glory.

2. **Honor God with the First fruits** – Abraham tithed before the law.

3. **Use Crisis for Increase** – Joseph prospered in famine.

4. **Blessings Follow Obedience** – Isaac sowed in famine and reaped 100-fold.

5. **Reputation Attracts Opportunity** – Boaz was known as upright and prosperous.

6. **Steward God's Resources** – David prepared wealth for a temple he wouldn't build.

7. **Reconciliation Releases Destiny** – Philemon's forgiveness propelled ministry.

8. **Be a Bridge, not a Barrier** – Cornelius opened the Gospel to nations.

9. **Vision Precedes Provision** – Jacob's dream set his entrepreneurial course.

10. **Discipline Protects Prosperity** – Hezekiah's preparation preserved legacy.

11. **Avoid the Trap of Hoarding** – The Rich Young Ruler kept wealth but lost purpose.

12. **God Will Elevate the Redeemed** – Rahab's faith made her royalty in Christ's lineage.

Appendix C: Reflection & Group Discussion Questions

1. Which biblical billionaire do you most identify with? Why?

2. How does your current view of wealth align with kingdom principles?

3. Have you ever missed a divine opportunity by holding onto money too tightly?

4. What legacy are you preparing for the next generation?

5. Are your financial decisions guided more by fear or by faith?

Use these questions in group study settings, mentorship circles, or personal journaling to **deepen the revelation** in this book.

Appendix D: Recommended Reading List

Books on Biblical Wealth & Stewardship:

- *Business Secrets from the Bible* – Rabbi Daniel Lapin

- *The Blessed Life* – Robert Morris

- *God, Money, and Me* – Paul de Jong

- *Money Mastery* – Billy Epperhart

- *Rich Church, Poor Church* – John Muratori

- *Thou Shall Prosper* – Rabbi Daniel Lapin

- *Poverty, Riches & Wealth* – Kris Vallotton

- *The Richest Man Who Ever Lived* – Steven K. Scott

- *Money, Possessions and Eternity* – Randy Alcorn

- *The Spirit of Leadership* – Dr. Myles Munroe

Appendix E: Recommended Websites & Platforms

Faith & Finance Resources:

- Crown Financial Ministries – Biblical principles for financial stewardship

- Dave Ramsey – Personal finance and debt elimination

- WealthBuilders.org – Kingdom entrepreneurship and real estate

- Generous Giving – Cultivating a lifestyle of radical generosity

- Kingdom Advisors – Christian financial planning and mentorship

Appendix F: Prayers for Kingdom Wealth Activation

1. **Prayer for Financial Wisdom**

    "Lord, grant me the wisdom of Solomon, not only to build wealth, but to manage it for Your glory."

2. **Prayer for Purposeful Prosperity**

    "May my resources serve Your Kingdom. Let my wealth fund souls, missions, and transformation."

3. **Prayer for Legacy Building**

    "Use me to set up a legacy of righteousness, stewardship, and generosity for generations after me."

4. **Prayer to Break Poverty Mindsets**

    "I renounce fear, greed, and scarcity thinking. I embrace the abundance of Heaven through faith."